Artificial Intelligence for Undergraduate Students

OrangeBooks Publication

1st Floor, Rajhans Arcade, Mall Road, Kohka, Bhilai, Chhattisgarh 490020

Website: **www.orangebooks.in**

© Copyright, 2025, Author

All rights reserved. No part of this book may be reproduced, stored in a retrieval system, or transmitted, in any form by any means, electronic, mechanical, magnetic, optical, chemical, manual, photocopying, recording or otherwise, without the prior written consent of its writer.

First Edition, 2025

ISBN: 978-93-6554-243-1

ARTIFICIAL INTELLIGENCE
FOR
UNDERGRADUATE STUDENTS

Dr. A.J.K. PRASAD
Dr. REDDAPPA H.N.

OrangeBooks Publication
www.orangebooks.in

Preface to the First Edition

It gives us immense pleasure to present the first edition of *"Artificial Intelligence for Undergraduate Students,"* a textbook designed to provide a comprehensive yet accessible introduction to the fascinating field of Artificial Intelligence (AI). This book has been structured with undergraduate students in mind, focusing on the core principles, theories, and applications of AI.

The textbook is organized into five chapters, each carefully designed to build a strong foundation and gradually introduce advanced topics. Special attention has been given to include relevant illustrations and tables that not only enhance understanding but also provide visual clarity to complex concepts. Additionally, each chapter concludes with a set of thoughtfully curated questions, encouraging students to reflect on and apply what they have learned.

Key Features of This Edition:
1. **Figures and Tables:** This first edition includes 30 figures and 14 tables, designed to simplify concepts and support visual learners. We have ensured high quality visual appeal and simple table formats. The hardbound copy contains black and white figures, while B\W images are provided in digital formats such as Amazon Kindle or e-book versions.

2. **Chapter Overviews and Summaries:** Each chapter begins with a concise overview, providing a roadmap of the topics covered, and concludes with a well-rounded summary and reflective questions to reinforce learning outcomes.

3. **End-of-Chapter Questions:** To support active learning, a set of review and application-based questions has been provided at the end of each chapter. These questions are designed to deepen understanding and encourage critical thinking about the covered subject matter.

4. **Indexing for Ease of Reference:** An alphabetical index and glossary are provided at the end of the book for reader convenience, enabling seamless navigation and quick reference to key terms and concepts.

5. **Chapter Breakdown:**

    - **Chapter 1: What is AI? Foundations and History of AI**

        This chapter lays the groundwork by exploring the origins, evolution, and foundational concepts of AI. It features 2 figures and 2 tables to support the narrative.

    - **Chapter 2: Agents and Environments - Intelligent Agents**

        A deep dive into intelligent agents, their environments, rationality, and related systems, supported by 10 figures and 2 tables.

    - **Chapter 3: Uncertain Knowledge and Reasoning**

        This chapter tackles the intricacies of dealing with uncertainty in AI, including probability, Bayes' rule, and inference techniques. It includes 4 figures and 1 table.

    - **Chapter 4: Search and Search Strategies**

        A detailed exploration of search algorithms, both uninformed and informed, along with logical agents, supported by 8 figures and 5 tables.

    - **Chapter 5: Knowledge-Based Agents**

        The final chapter explores knowledge representation, logic, and reasoning techniques with 6 figures and 3 tables.

The collective effort behind this textbook reflects our commitment to academic excellence and fostering a deeper understanding of AI concepts among undergraduate students.

We sincerely hope that this book will serve as a valuable resource for students and educators alike. Constructive feedback from readers is always welcome as we strive to improve and adapt this book to meet evolving educational needs.

It is worth mentioning that all figures in the textbook have been redrawn using licensed software. We gratefully acknowledge the use of two icons in Figure 4.1, which have been properly credited in the text.

Sincerely,

The Authors

Acknowledgement

Firstly, we would like to thank the almighty for providing us an opportunity to write this book. We express our heartfelt thanks to the management of Don Bosco Institute of Technology and the management of **Rajya Vokkaligara Sangha**, Bengaluru.

We would like to express our gratitude to **Dr. B.S. Nagabhushana**, Principal, Don Bosco Institute of Technology and **Dr.Aswath M U,** Principal, Bangalore Institute of Technology, Bengaluru.

We are especially thankful to our family members **Mrs. Dharani S, Diganth R, Venkata Lakshmi, Aparna and Jyotsna**, for their continuous support and encouragement for their understanding in our endeavour.

Our indebted thanks to our colleagues, for their encouragement and support rendered from time to time.

We are grateful to **Orange Books Publishing** (Orangebooks.in) for bringing out this book in this elegant format and our special thanks to **Mdhavai, Payal Ghosh,** and their team for the editorial support.

Dr. A.J.K. PRASAD

Dr. REDDAPPA H.N.

Contents

Preface to the First Edition .... *v*
Acknowledgement .... *viii*
List of Figures .... *x*
List of Tables .... *xi*

Chapter - 1
Introduction to Artificial Intelligence 1

Chapter - 2
Agents And Environments 25

Chapter - 3
Uncertain Knowledge and Reasoning 74

Chapter - 4
Search and Search Strategies 98

Chapter - 5
Knowledge Based Agents and Logical Reasoning 133

Chapter Wise Questions *185*
Index *190*
Glossary *193*

List of Figures

Figure 1.1 Artificial Intelligence 2
Figure 1.2 Foundations of Artificial Intelligence 3
Figure 2.1 Types of AI Agents 31
Figure 2.2 Simple Reflex Agent 33
Figure 2.3 Model-Based Reflex Agent 34
Figure 2.4 Utility-Based Reflex Agent 41
Figure 2.5 Learning Agent 44
Figure 2.6 Multi-Agent Systems 51
Figure 2.7 Chatbot (Image generated using Free AI Image Generator:
   Text to Image Online) 65
Figure 2.8 Expert Systems (Image generated using Free AI Image
   Generator: Text to Image Online) 68
Figure 2.9 Expert Systems 69
Figure 2.10 Expert Systems with Expert System Shell 69
Figure 3.1 Probability of an Event Scale 87
Figure 3.2 Sample space, Events, their complements, unions,
   intersections, and independent events 89
Figure 3.3 Conditional Probability 90
Figure 3.4 Decomposing Joint Probabilities 92
Figure 4.1 Types of Search Algorithms in AI 101
Figure 4.2 Breadth-First Search 105
Figure 4.3 Depth First Search 107
Figure 4.4 Depth-Limited Search. 109
Figure 4.5 Iterative Deepening Depth-First Search (IDDFS) 112
Figure 4.6 Greedy Best first search graph 119
Figure 4.7 Evaluation function f(n) in A* Algorithm 122
Figure 4.8 8-Puzzle: Initial State and Possible Moves 129
Figure 5.1 The Knowledge-Based Agent Architecture 136
Figure 5.2 The Wumpus World (4x4 grid) 140
Figure 5.3 Logical Connectives of Propositional Logic 146
Figure 5.4 Basic First-Order Logic Elements 151
Figure 5.5 Forward Chaining 175
Figure 5.6 Backward Chaining 178

List of Tables

Table 1.1: Multidisciplinary Skills and Domains in Artificial Intelligence 5

Table 1.2 Four Perspectives of Artificial Intelligence (source Russell and Norvig) 7

Table 2.1 Various Environments in AI 58

Table 2.2 Presents a Summary with G Examples of Environments in AI and The Corresponding PEAS (Performance, Environment, Actuators, Sensors) For Agents 62

Table 3.1 Joint distribution two variables X(Rain) and B(Traffic) 91

Table 4.1 Comparison to Depth-First Search with Depth Limited Search 111

Table 4.2 Comparison of IDDFS with Other Algorithms 115

Table 4.3 Comparison of Bidirectional DFS with Other Algorithms 118

Table 4.4 Comparison of GBFS with Other Algorithms 121

Table 4.5 Comparison of A* with Other Algorithms 126

Table 4.6 Comparison of Search Algorithms for Solving the 8 Puzzle Problem 129

Table 5.1 Summary for First-Order Logic Components 153

Table 5.2 Propositional Inference and First-Order Inference 163

Table 5.3 Specialised Techniques used in FOL 166

Chapter – 1
Introduction to Artificial Intelligence

> Artificially created Intelligence (AI)is the science of creating machines that think and act like humans or human beings, having foundations in computer science, mathematics, psychology, and linguistics. With significant studies in disciplines/subjects covering natural language processing, machine learning, robotics, and computer vision, AI will have evolved from early fundamental principles to innovative triumphs by 2024, changing industries and our daily life.

Artificial Intelligence (AI) refers to the simulation of human intelligence in machines that are Artificial Intelligence (AI) refers to the simulation of human intelligence in machines that are programmed to think and act like humans. It involves the development of algorithms and computer programs that can perform tasks that typically require human intelligence, such as visual perception, speech recognition, decision-making, and language translation. AI has the potential to revolutionize many industries and has a wide range of applications, from virtual personal assistants to AI agents Multi-Agent Systems to self-driving cars.

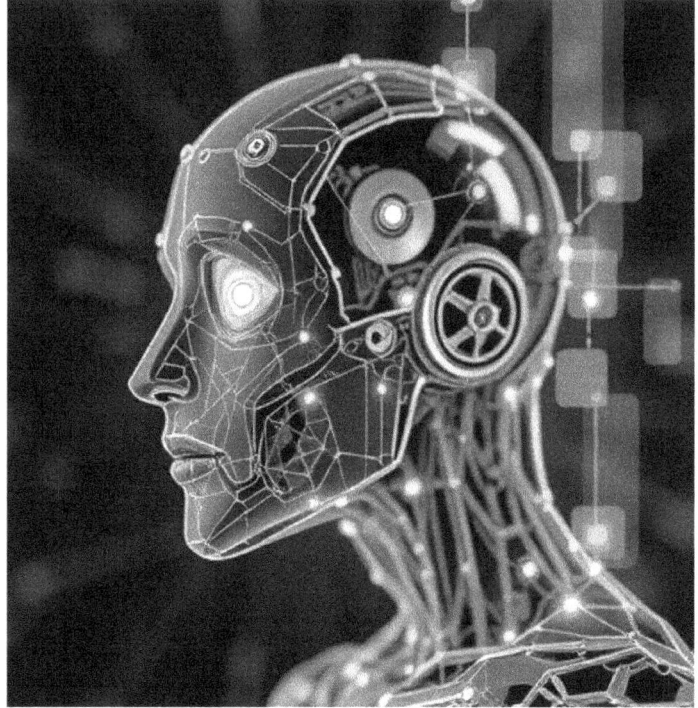

Figure 1.1 Artificial Intelligence

(Figure generated from the webpage https://deepai.org)

It is appropriate to understand the meaning of artificial intelligence before delving into the subject of Artificial Intelligence. Let us first understand the meaning of intelligence:

1.1 The four kingdoms: mineral, plant, animal, and human kingdoms.

The intellectual capacity of the mineral kingdom is low, plants display considerable intelligence through their capacity to grow and reproduce. Animals show more advancement through qualities that include growth, reproduction, and mobility. Among all of these kingdoms, humans surpass the others in intelligence, creativity, invention, and being able to use the other three for benefiting society.

1.1.2 Intelligence: Intelligence has been defined in a number of ways, encompassing being able to abstract, logic, understand self-awareness, learn, understand feelings reason, plan, be creative, think critically, and handle problems. It can be described as the ability to gain or infer information and retain it as knowledge that can be applied to adaptive behaviours within an environment or environment.

1.2 Multidisciplinary Nature and foundations of Artificial Intelligence

Artificial intelligence (AI) is in essence multidisciplinary, combining concepts and approaches from a number of domains to build systems that imitate human intelligence. It combines together principles from computer science for algorithm design, math for logic and optimization, neurology for cognitive processes, psychology for behaviour modelling, linguistics for language comprehension, and philosophy for ethical and philosophical issues. This dynamic interplay of disciplines not only improves AI's capabilities, but also assures that its applications are resilient, flexible and adaptive, and in line with different demands from humans. Let's delve into the multidisciplinary nature of AI\ and foundations of AI

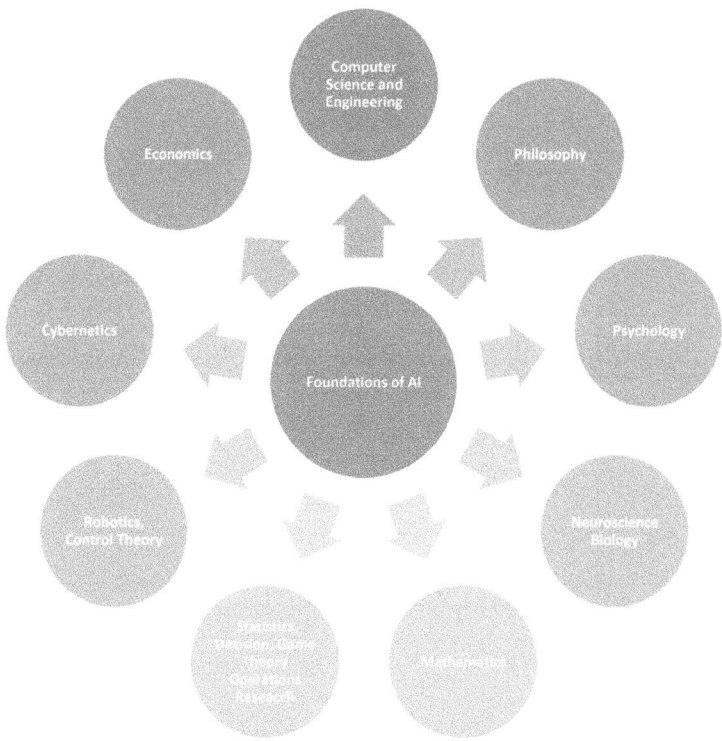

Figure 1.2 Foundations of Artificial Intelligence

1.2.1 Multidisciplinary Approach of Artificial Intelligence

Artificial intelligence (AI) is a broad, multidisciplinary field that expands far beyond traditional computer science. It combines various engineering and scientific disciplines to create intelligent computers capable of executing complex tasks. Rather than being limited to computational approaches, AI encompasses an extensive number of technologies and strategies for replicating intelligent behavior across different platforms and physical systems. Artificial intelligence's primary goal is to build systems that imitate or replicate human intelligence in order to efficiently carry out activities like thinking, learning, and problem solving. Let's now explore the various disciplines and domain knowledge required for effectively engaging in the world of AI.

1. **Computer Science.**

algorithmic design and software development Machine Learning and Data Processing Advanced computational approaches.

2. **Robotics.**

Physical system design Mechanical Engineering Sensor Integration autonomous movement and manipulation.

3. **Control Engineering.**

System Dynamics and Feedback Mechanisms Adaptive Control Strategies Optimization of mechanical and electrical systems. Precision control and decision-making algorithms

4. **Cognitive science.**

Understanding Human Intelligence Neural network modelling. Cognitive processing simulation Learning and adaption processes In the table 1.1 is presented are the multidisciplinary skills required for understanding the AI systems and domain expertise team requirement for designing, testing, and deploying AI systems.

Table 1.1: Multidisciplinary Skills and Domains in Artificial Intelligence

Domain Category	Technological Domains	Key Technologies	Practical Applications	Core Capabilities
Intelligence Types	Computational Intelligence	• Software Algorithms	• Data Processing Systems	• Logical Reasoning
	• Mechanical Intelligence	• Physical System Design	• Robotic Mechanisms	• Structural Adaptation
	• Sensory Intelligence	• Perception Systems	•Environmental Interaction	• Real-time Analysis
	• Adaptive Intelligence	• Learning Algorithms	• Self-improvement Mechanisms	• Dynamic Reconfiguration
Autonomous Systems	• Vehicle Automation	• Sensor Fusion	• Self-driving Cars	• Independent Navigation
	• Unmanned Vehicles	• AI Navigation	• UAVs	• Autonomous Operation
	• Industrial Robotics	• Precision Control	• Automation Robots	• Intelligent Manufacturing
Smart Infrastructure	• Traffic Management	• Real-time Data Processing	• Adaptive Traffic Systems	• Optimization
	• Energy Systems	• Predictive Analytics	• Smart Grid Technologies	• Resource Efficiency
	• Building Management	• IoT Integration	• Intelligent Facility Control	• Automated Maintenance
Advanced Robotics	• Medical Robotics	• Precision Mechanics	• Surgical Robots	• Minimally Invasive Procedures
	• Exploration Robotics	• Rugged Design	•Planetary/ Deep Sea Robots	• Extreme Environment Operation
	•Collaborative Robotics	• Human-Robot Interaction	• Industrial Collaborative Robots	• Safe Interaction

Sensing Technologies	• Multi-modal Sensors	• Advanced Detection	• Real-time Perception	• Environmental Understanding
	• Precision Measurement	• High-resolution Sensing	• Accurate Data Acquisition	• Detailed Observation
Processing Technologies	• Distributed Computing	• Parallel Processing	• Complex Computation	• Scalable Performance
	• Edge Computing	• Localized Processing	• Low-latency Systems	• Immediate Response
	• Neuromorphic Computing	• Brain-inspired Architecture	• Adaptive Processing	• Intelligent Computation
Actuating Technologies	• Precision Motor Control	• Servo Mechanisms	• Robotic Movement	• Accurate Positioning
	• Adaptive Mechanisms	• Force Feedback Systems	• Dynamic Response	• Responsive Interaction
Emerging Paradigms	• Cyber-Physical Systems	• Integrated Computing	• Real-time Monitoring	• Seamless Interaction
	• Hybrid Intelligence Systems	• Biological-Artificial Fusion	• Collaborative Frameworks	• Enhanced Capabilities
Critical Challenges	• Skill Integration	• Multidisciplinary Expertise	• Complex System Design	• Holistic Understanding
	• Ethical Considerations	• Safety Protocols	• Responsible Innovation	• Transparent Operations
	• System Reliability	• Performance Predictability	• Consistent Functionality	

1.3 Definitions of AI

The Oxford Dictionary definition: "The theory and development of computer systems able to perform tasks normally requiring human intelligence, such as visual perception, speech recognition, decision-making, and translation between languages."

1. **John McCarthy (1955):** "AI is the science and engineering of making intelligent machines."

2. **Stuart Russell and Peter Norvig (2003):** "AI is the study of agents that receive percepts from the environment and take actions to maximize their chances of achieving their goals."

3. **Elaine Rich (1983):** "Artificial intelligence is the study of how to make computers do things which, at the moment, people do better."

Table 1.2 Four Perspectives of Artificial Intelligence (source Russell and Norvig)

		Definitions based on Thinking		
Measure success by adhering to human performance standards.	Perspective	Human-like Intelligence	"Ideal" Intelligent/Rational	Compares actual performance to an ideal standard.
	Thought/Reasoning	Thinking Humanly	Thinking Rationally	
	Behaviour/Actions	Acting Humanly	Acting Rationally	
		Definitions based on Behaviour		

Let's now explore the definitions as envisioned by different scents

1. **Explanations. Thinking Humanly:** The ability of machines to think like humans, mimicking human cognitive processes. "The exciting new effort to make computers think ... machines with minds, in the

full and literal sense." (Haugeland, 1985) & "[The automation of] activities that we associate with human thinking, activities such as decision-making, problem solving, learning ..." (Bellman, 1978)

2. **Thinking Rationally**: The logical reasoning approach where machines aim to think according to ideal rationality. "The study of mental faculties through the use of computational models." (Charniak and McDermott, 1985) & The study of the computations that make it possible to perceive, reason, and act." (Winston, 1992)

3. **Acting Humanly** Machines perform actions that imitate human behavior (e.g., passing the Turing Test). "The art of creating machines that perform functions that require intelligence when performed by people." (Kurzweil, 1990) & "The study of how to make computers do things at which, at the moment, people are better." (Rich and Knight, 1991) &

4. **Acting Rationally**: Machines act to achieve the best outcome or an optimal performance measure based on rationality. "Computational Intelligence is the study of the design of intelligent agents." (Poole et al., 1998) & the intelligent behavior in artifacts." (Nilsson, 1998)

Today, modern dictionary definitions highlight AI as a subfield of computer science and how machines might mimic human intellect (being human-like rather than being human).

Evolution and key areas of AI research and development:

Key Research Domains in Artificial Intelligence and Machine Learning

Artificial Intelligence and Machine Learning have evolved into several specialized fields of study and application:

1. **Computer Vision**
   - Image recognition and processing
   - Object detection and tracking
   - Scene understanding and analysis

2. **Speech and Text Technologies**
   - Speech recognition and synthesis
   - Text analysis and processing
   - Voice-based interactions

3. **Deep Learning**
   - Neural network architectures
   - Pattern recognition
   - Feature extraction and learning

4. **Natural Language Processing**
   - Large Language Models (LLMs)
   - Advanced text generation
   - Complex reasoning capabilities
   - Broad knowledge integration
   - **Small Language Models (SLMs)**

4.2 Task-specific applications
   - Efficient resource utilization
   - Specialized domain expertise

1.4.1 Classification of Artificial Intelligence Based on Capabilities

Narrow/Weak AI (ANI)
   - Designed for specific tasks
   - Cannot extend beyond programmed domains
   - Currently prevalent in real-world applications

- Examples: virtual assistants, game AI, recommendation systems

General AI (AGI)

- Human-level cognitive abilities
- Capability to understand and learn any intellectual task
- Currently theoretical
- Goal of matching human intelligence across domains

Super AI (ASI)

- Exceeds human cognitive capabilities
- Theoretical concept
- Potential for recursive self-improvement
- Subject of future AI research and ethics discussions

1.4.2 Based on Functionality

1. **Reactive Machines**
   - Basic AI systems
   - Respond to immediate inputs
   - No memory or past experience usage
   - Example: chess-playing computers

2. **Limited Memory**
   - Uses past experiences
   - Temporary memory storage
   - Learning from historical data
   - Example: self-driving vehicles

3. **Theory of Mind**
   - ❖ Understanding beliefs, intentions
   - ❖ Social interaction capability
   - ❖ Currently under development
   - ❖ Aimed at human-like social intelligence

4. **Self-Aware**
   - ❖ Consciousness and self-awareness
   - ❖ Understanding own existence
   - ❖ Purely theoretical concept
   - ❖ Ultimate goal of AI development

1.4.3 Based on Technology

1. **Machine Learning**
   - ❖ Pattern recognition
   - ❖ Data-based learning
   - ❖ Algorithmic improvement
   - ❖ Supervised and unsupervised learning

Deep Learning
   - ❖ Neural network based
   - ❖ Multiple processing layers
   - ❖ Complex pattern recognition
   - ❖ Automated feature extraction

Expert Systems
   - ❖ Rule-based decision making
   - ❖ Domain-specific knowledge
   - ❖ Logical inference engines
   - ❖ Human expertise simulation

1.4.4 Based on Applications

1. **Industrial AI**
   - Manufacturing optimization
   - Quality control
   - Process automation
   - Predictive maintenance

Consumer AI
   - Personal assistants
   - Smart home devices
   - Entertainment systems
   - Recommendation engines

Business AI
   - Decision support systems
   - Customer service bots
   - Market analysis
   - Risk assessment

Scientific AI
   - Research assistance
   - Data analysis
   - Scientific discovery
   - Hypothesis generation

1.4.5 Based on Learning Approach

1. **Supervised Learning**
   - Labelled data training
   - Predictive modelling
   - Classification tasks

- ❖ Regression analysis

Unsupervised Learning
- ❖ Pattern discovery
- ❖ Clustering
- ❖ Dimensionality reduction
- ❖ Anomaly detection

Reinforcement Learning
- ❖ Trial and error learning
- ❖ Reward-based systems
- ❖ Dynamic adaptation
- ❖ Environment interaction

Semi-supervised Learning
- ❖ Partial labelled data
- ❖ Hybrid approach
- ❖ Cost-effective learning
- ❖ Practical applications

1.4.6 Based on Implementation

1. **Software-based AI**
- ❖ Computer programs
- ❖ Cloud services
- ❖ Virtual environments
- ❖ Digital platforms

Hardware-based AI
- ❖ Specialized processors
- ❖ Neural hardware
- ❖ AI accelerators

- Quantum computing integration

Hybrid AI
- Combined approaches
- Multiple technologies
- Integrated systems
- Enhanced capabilities

This classification system provides a comprehensive framework for understanding the various dimensions and approaches in artificial intelligence, each indexed for easy reference and organization.

1.5 A Brief History of Artificial Intelligence

Early Foundations (1940s-1950s)

The Turing Era
- Alan Turing's 1950 paper introduced "thinking machine" concept
- Development of Turing Test for machine intelligence evaluation
- Early computational foundations established

Birth of AI (1956)
- Dartmouth Conference milestone
- John McCarthy coins "Artificial Intelligence"
- Establishment of AI as formal research field

Pioneering Years (1950s-1970s)
- Development of symbolic AI systems
- Creation of Logic Theorist
- Implementation of General Problem Solver (GPS)

AI Winter Period (1970s-1980s)
- Funding reductions
- Technical limitations
- Reduced research momentum

Expert Systems Era (1980s)

- Development of MYCIN and DENDRAL
- Industrial applications emerge
- Rule-based decision systems

Machine Learning Evolution (1990s-2000s)
- Transition to data-driven approaches
- Statistical method advancement
- Computing power increases

Modern AI Revolution (2010s-Present)
- Deep learning breakthrough
- Neural network advancement
- Integration into daily technology

Significant Milestones

1950s
- Turing's seminal paper (1950)
- Dartmouth Conference (1956)

1970s-1990s
- MYCIN development (1976)
- Expert systems emergence

2000s-Present
- Deep Blue victory (1997)
- Watson on Jeopardy! (2011)
- AlphaGo achievement (2016)
- Generative AI emergence (2020s)

Contemporary Applications

Healthcare
- Medical diagnosis
- Drug discovery
- Personalized treatment

Financial Services
- Fraud detection
- Trading algorithms
- Risk assessment

Transportation
- Autonomous vehicles
- Traffic optimization
- Navigation systems

Educational Technology
- Adaptive learning
- Intelligent tutoring
- Educational assessment

Entertainment Industry
- Content recommendation
- Gaming AI
- Visual effects

1. **Modern AI Revolution (2010s-2024)**

2. **Deep Learning Breakthroughs**
   - Convolutional Neural Networks (CNNs)
   - Transformer architecture introduction (2017)
   - BERT and language model evolution

3. **Large Language Models Era**
   - GPT series evolution (GPT-1 to GPT-4)
   - Claude and other advanced AI assistants

- Open source LLMs emergence

4. **Multimodal AI Development**
   - DALL-E, Midjourney, Stable Diffusion Text-to-Image Models
   - Text-to-video generation
   - Speech synthesis advancement

5. **Latest Milestones (2020-2024)**

   2020
   - GPT-3 demonstrates advanced language capabilities
   - AlphaFold 2 revolutionizes protein structure prediction

   2021
   - DALL-E introduces text-to-image generation
   - Codex demonstrates code generation capabilities

   2022
   - ChatGPT launches, marking mass AI adoption
   - Stable Diffusion opens source for image generation

   2023
   - GPT-4 shows multimodal capabilities
   - Claude 2 and advanced AI assistants emerge
   - Open source LLMs gain prominence Open Source AI

   Early 2024
   - Anthropic's Claude 3 models

- Multimodal and video generation advances
- Enhanced reasoning capabilities in AI systems

Emerging Technologies

6. **Advanced AI Architectures**
   - Mixture of Experts (MoE) models
   - Sparse neural networks
   - Efficient transformer variants

7. **Specialized AI Systems**
   - Small Language Models (SLMs) Small Language Models
   - Domain-specific AI models
   - Edge AI implementations

8. **AI Infrastructure**
   - Quantum computing integration
   - Neuromorphic hardware
   - AI accelerator chips

9. **Contemporary Applications**

[Previous applications section remains, with these additions:]

10. **Scientific Research**
    - Drug discovery
    - Climate modelling
    - Materials science

11. Creative Industries

- Content generation
- Design assistance
- Music composition

12. Business Intelligence

- Predictive analytics
- Process automation
- Decision support systems

13. Multi-Agent Systems and Agentic AI

Overview of Agentic AI

- Autonomous decision-making capabilities
- Goal-oriented behavior
- Self-directed task completion
- Proactive problem-solving

Multi-Agent Architectures

14. Collaborative Frameworks

- Agent-to-agent communication
- Task distribution and coordination
- Collective problem-solving
- Emergent behavior patterns

15. Key Components

- Autonomous agents with specialized roles
- Communication protocols
- Resource management
- Conflict resolution mechanisms

16. Current Research Directions

Microsoft AutoGen

- **Framework for building agent-based applications**
- Multiple conversational agents
- Customizable agent behaviours

17. Open-source development **Reference: https://microsoft.github.io/autogen/**

18. **Anthropic's Constitutional AI**

- Value-aligned agent behavior
- Ethical decision-making frameworks

19. **Controlled autonomy Reference: https://www.anthropic.com/research**

20. **Google DeepMind's GOAT Framework**

- Goal-oriented agent teams
- Complex task coordination
- Scalable agent interactions **Reference: https://deepmind.google/discover/blog/**

21. **Applications**

    Business Process Automation

    - Workflow optimization
    - Resource allocation
    - Intelligent task routing **Reference:** https://research.ibm.com/blog/ai-agents

22. **Virtual Assistants Evolution**

    - Beyond simple chatbots
    - Context-aware interactions

23. Proactive assistance **Reference:** https://www.gartner.com/en/topics/artificial-intelligence

24. **Scientific Research**

    - Drug discovery optimization
    - Climate modelling
    - Materials science **Reference:** https://www.nature.com/articles/s41586-021-03819-2

25. **Emerging Trends**

    Autonomous Agent Networks

    - Self-organizing systems
    - Distributed decision-making
    - Adaptive behavior **Reference:** https://arxiv.org/abs/2304.03442

26. Human-Agent Collaboration

- Interactive problem-solving
- Augmented intelligence
- Trust-based interactions **Reference:** https://www.frontiersin.org/articles/10.3389/frobt.2020.00053/full

27. Challenges and Considerations

28. Technical Challenges

- Coordination complexity
- Scalability issues
- Performance optimization **Reference:** https://ai.stanford.edu/blog/autonomous-agents/

29. Ethical Considerations

- Decision transparency
- Accountability
- Safety protocols **Reference:** https://hai.stanford.edu/news/ethical-considerations-ai-agents

30. Future Directions

- Advanced Capabilities
- Enhanced reasoning
- Dynamic adaptation
- Improved collaboration

31. Integration Areas

- Smart cities
- Healthcare systems
- Financial markets
- Educational platforms

Note: The subject of artificial intelligence is continually evolving, with new research, breakthroughs, and applications. For the latest concepts and developments, recent publications from authentic sources such as the National Science Foundation (NSF), academic institutions, and industry leaders. These sources provide current news on AI developments, ethical/moral concerns, and societal implications, ensuring an in-depth comprehension of this dynamic and changing field of Artificial Intelligence.

Chapter Summary and Concluding Thoughts

In this chapter, we explored the basic concepts, multidisciplinary nature, and evolution of Artificial Intelligence. We began with a broad introduction, diving into the fundamentals of AI and its transformative potential. The four kingdoms of intelligence provide a framework for distinguishing and categorizing different manifestations of intelligence, allowing to more clearly understand AI's capabilities in relation to human and natural intelligence. We subsequently looked at the multidisciplinary characteristics of AI and its core disciplines, which include computer science, mathematics, cognitive science, and other fields, emphasizing the broad knowledge needed to advance in this subject. This naturally led to a discussion of the multidisciplinary skills needed for capturing AI systems and the importance of domain expertise for developing, evaluating, and launching AI systems effectively.

Building on this, we explored different definitions of artificial intelligence, demonstrating its enormous reach and various points of view from which it might be comprehended. The chapter then discussed the key research areas in AI and machine learning emphasizing how modern successes evolved from long-standing obstacles. We also investigated the classification of AI systems, which offered insight into how AI technologies are categorized based on their design and usefulness. Finally, we traced the history of AI covering its evolution from the early conceptual stages to the groundbreaking achievements of 2024, which have ushered in a new era of transformative technologies.

Chapter – 2
Agents And Environments

> Agents and Environments- Intelligent Agents: Agents and environment, Concept of Rationality, The nature of environment, The structure of agents. Chatbots- Expert Systems: Representing and using domain knowledge, ES shells.

Introduction

Agents in the context of Artificial Intelligence

Agents in the context of artificial intelligence, are fundamentally independent systems that can do a variety of activities on their own, such as answering consumer questions, evaluating large datasets, and making suggestions.

In today's rapidly evolving digital ecosystems, AI agents' ability to perceive, reason, learn, and act autonomously drives technological progress. These innovative tools have the ability to interrupt industries like medical care, banking, entertainment, and logistics. More than just technological successes, AI agents represent a significant shift in society structures, increasing productivity and opening up new avenues for human-computer collaboration. Their growth reflects not only technological advancements, but also the future of our increasingly interconnected world. Gaining an enhanced understanding of their evolution is critical—not only for technology enthusiasts, but for anyone who is interested in shaping the future of our digital era.

In contrast to traditional software, AI agents have the capacity to learn, adapt, and improve their performance over time. For Gen Z entrepreneurs, who emphasize efficiency, automation, and customized experiences, AI agents serve as a revolutionary instrument capable of revolutionizing their operations.

A human agent has sensory organs, namely eyes, ears, nose, tongue, and skin, similar to sensors, and also effectors such as hands, legs, and mouth.

A robotic agent combines cameras and infrared range finders with sensors, and utilizes various motors and actuators as effectors.

A software agent uses encoded bit strings for its programming and actions.

In today's rapidly advancing digital landscape, AI agents are driving technological innovation with their ability to perceive, reason, learn, and act autonomously. These transformative tools have the potential to revolutionize industries ranging from healthcare and finance to entertainment and logistics. More than just technical achievements, AI agents represent a profound shift in societal structures, offering enhanced productivity and unlocking new possibilities for human-computer collaboration. Their evolution reflects not only advancements in technology but also the direction of our increasingly interconnected world. Gaining a deeper understanding of their development is essential— not just for technology enthusiasts but for anyone invested in shaping the future of our digital era.

Let's now delve into the origin and need for development of agents in artificial intelligence.

Key Characteristics of AI Agents:
1. **Autonomy** Agents operate without human intervention, making decisions based on their programming or learned behavior.
2. **Perception**: They observe the environment through sensors (physical or digital inputs like cameras, microphones, or APIs).
3. **Action**: Agents interact with their environment using actuators or system commands.

4. **Rationality**: They aim to take actions that maximize their performance measure based on their goals and knowledge.

Importance of AI Agents:
AI agents are essential to fostering automation and decision-making because they imitate intelligent behavior to enhance the connection between technology and human needs. Here's why they matter:

1. **Automation of Complex Tasks:**
    - AI agents automate repetitive or high-stakes tasks, such as autonomous driving and diagnosis in medicine.

2. **Scalability:**
    - Search engines and recommendation systems can handle large amounts of data and actions simultaneously.

3. **Improved Decision-Making:**
    - Agents improve decision-making efficiency by evaluating environments and performing real-time actions, leading to faster and more accurate decisions.

4. **Learning and Adaptation:**
    - Adaptive agents build knowledge over time, making them invaluable in dynamic industries such as banking, e-commerce, and logistics.

5. **Human-AI Collaboration:**
    - Chatbots
    - and similar AI agents can help humans with customer assistance and data analysis, boosting productivity.

6. **Foundation for Advanced AI Systems:**
    - AI agents act as a foundation for advanced AI systems, such as multi-agent systems and general AI.

Understanding AI Agents:
Understanding AI agents allows developers to design systems that are efficient and optimized for specific contexts.

7. Moral issues include long-term societal impact and user safety.

8. Build trust through transparent decision-making.

In short, AI agents are the foundation of intelligent systems, pushing advancements in automation, adaptability, and complicated issue resolution. Understanding the roles and functions of artificial intelligence's fundamental elements is critical for achieving its full potential.

The Origins and Development of Agents in AI

Historical Context and Motivation
Early Foundations (1950s-1960s)

The concept of agents in AI emerged from the early vision of creating machines that could interact intelligently with their environment. During the 1950s, pioneers like Alan Turing and John McCarthy contemplated the possibility of machines that could sense, reason, and act. The fundamental motivation was to create systems that could:

1. Operate autonomously in complex environments
2. Make decisions without constant human intervention
3. Learn from experience and adapt their behaviour.

Theoretical Development (1970s-1980s):
The formal development of agent theory was driven by several key realizations:

1. **Limitations of Traditional Programs**

    - Traditional programs were too rigid and couldn't handle dynamic environments
    - They lacked the ability to adapt to changing circumstances
    - They required explicit programming for every possible situation.

2. Need for Autonomous Systems

- Growing complexity of computational tasks demanded more autonomous solutions.
- Industrial and military applications required systems that could operate independently.
- Space exploration necessitated robots that could function with minimal human supervision.

Key Motivating Factors

1. Environmental Interaction

Agents were conceived to address the fundamental challenge of creating systems that could effectively interact with their environment:

- Sensing: The ability to perceive and interpret environmental conditions.
- Acting: The capability to take actions that affect the environment.
- Feedback: The capacity to understand the results of actions taken

2. Goal-Oriented Behaviour

The agent paradigm provided a framework for implementing goal-directed behaviour:

- Systems could be designed with specific objectives
- Actions could be evaluated based on their contribution to goals
- Complex tasks could be broken down into manageable sub-goals

3. Adaptability Requirements

The need for adaptive systems drove the development of learning agents:

- Systems that could improve performance through experience
- Ability to handle unexpected situations

- Capacity to operate in partially unknown environments

Theoretical Foundations for AI Agents

1. Decision Theory

Agent development was influenced by decision theory, which provided:

- Framework for rational decision-making under uncertainty
- Methods for evaluating alternative actions
- Techniques for optimizing outcomes

2. Control Theory

Control theory contributed essential concepts:

- Feedback mechanisms
- State estimation
- Stability analysis

3. Cognitive Science

Insights from cognitive science shaped agent development:

- Models of human decision-making
- Problem-solving strategies
- Learning mechanisms

Types of AI Agents:
In figure 2.1 types of agents is given.

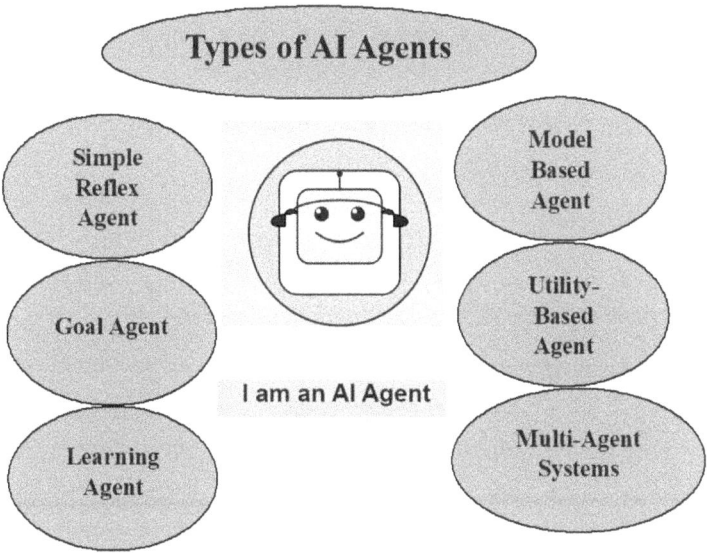

Figure 2.1 Types of AI Agents

1. **Simple Reflex Agents**

These agents operate based on a set of predefined rules that map percepts directly to actions. They are suitable for static environments but fail in dynamic or complex settings because they lack memory or learning capabilities.

Basic Reflex Agents

1. **Definition:** A set of predefined condition-action rules, or if-then statements, control how simple reflex agents act/behave.

2. **Features:**
    - ❖ Directly respond to perceptions without maintaining an internal state.
    - ❖ Ideal for environments that are static and fully observable.
    - ❖ Lack the ability to learn or retain information.

Examples:
1. **Thermostat Example:** A thermostat activates heating when the temperature drops below a certain point

   Spam Email Filter: A classic instance of a simple reflex agent is a spam email filter.

Spam Email Filter

A spam email filter exemplifies the fundamental characteristics of artificial intelligence's reflex-based decision-making.

- **Mechanism of Perception and Action**
  1. After reading incoming emails, the filter automatically categorizes them using pre-established condition-action rules.
  2. Importantly, this system does not take historical data into account.
  3. It does not analyse trends in previous email content or consider the sender's past behaviour.

- **Making Actions Based on Rules**
  1. If the subject section of an email contains specific trigger words or phrases (such as "buy now," "free," or "discount"), it is classified as spam.
  2. Mark as spam if the sender's address is listed in the spammer database.
  3. Classify as non-spam if the sender originates from a verified legitimate source.

Agent Classification

There are two main reasons why the spam filter is an example of a basic reflex agent:

1. It makes inferences based solely on perceptions of the present (the sender and the content of the email).

2. It cannot:
   i. Examine past email trends
   ii. Use previous categories to learn
   iii. Alter its criteria for decision-making over time

The spam email filter illustrates fundamental concepts of reflex-based artificial intelligence systems,

4. **Stimulus-Response Mechanism:** Highlights the system's efficiency in basic decision-making tasks and its intrinsic limitations in handling complex, context-dependent scenarios.

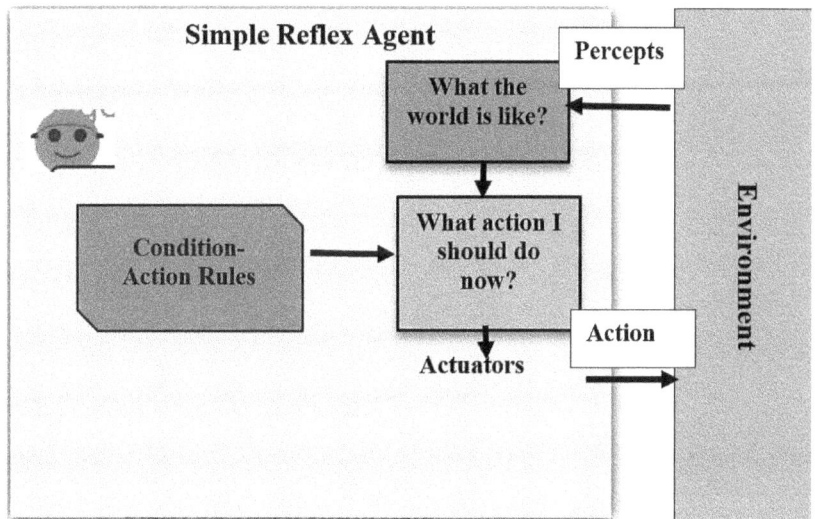

Figure 2.2 Simple Reflex Agent

2. **Model-Based Reflex Agents**

Model Based Agents build and maintain an internal model of the environment, which helps them keep track of changes over time. By using this model, they can handle partially observable environments partially observable environments more effectively compared to simple reflex agents.

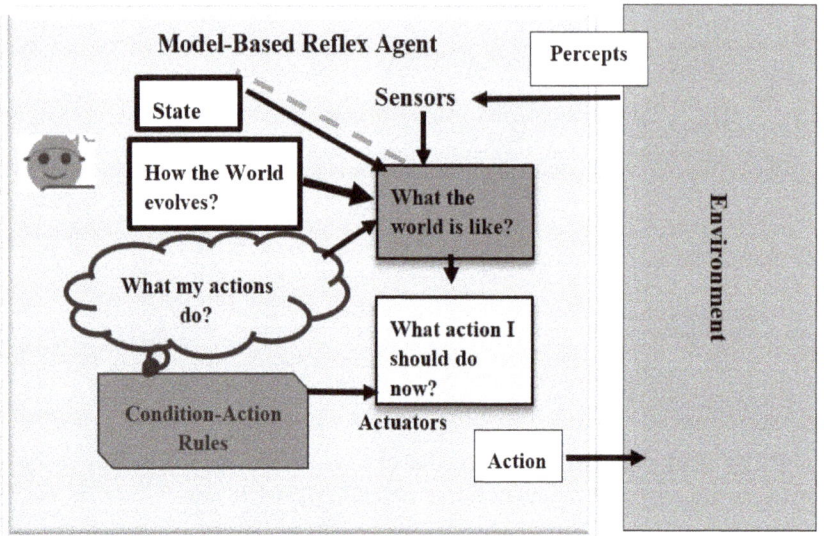

Figure 2.3 Model-Based Reflex Agent

Overview of the Architecture

By maintaining an internal state of their environment, model-based agents exhibit an advanced form of agent development. These systems, in contrast to basic reflex agents, use two essential models: a transition model and a world model.

Main Components

State Tracker

- Maintains the world as it is.
- Updates in view of new perspectives.
- Incorporates previous information.

World Model

- Depicts the way in which the world changes/evolves.
- Provides rules for the dynamics of the environment.
- Illustrates how actions and results are interrelated.

Model of Transition
- Predicts how choices will affect the environment.
- Anticipates possible outcomes based on actions alongside current situations.
- Handles prediction uncertainty.

Operational Mechanism
Processing of Information

Phase of Perception
- Sensory input is provided to the agent.
- Internal state representation is updated.
- Combines updated information into the present model.

State Update Phase:
- Combines data from sensors with the prior state.
- Fulfills the world model's criteria.
- Keeps internal representation consistent.

The Phase of Action Selection
- Utilizes the transition model for predicting results.
- Evaluates various options of action.
- Selects the best course of action based on predictions.

Advantages of Model Based Agent

Enhanced Decision Making
- ❖ Better handling of partial observability.
- ❖ Improved prediction capabilities.
- ❖ More robust action selection.

- **Environmental Adaptation**
  - ❖ Learns from experience.
  - ❖ Updates internal models.
  - ❖ Handles dynamic environments.

Implementation Example

- Autonomous Vehicle Navigation

3. Goal-Based Agents:

These agents choose actions based on achieving specific goals. Instead of just reacting to the environment, they evaluate possible future states to ensure their actions align with their objectives. This makes them more flexible and intelligent.

Goal-Based Agents: Understanding Purpose-Driven AI

Fundamental Principles

Goal-based agents represent a more sophisticated approach to artificial intelligence, incorporating explicit goals to guide their decision-making process Unlike simpler agent types, these systems evaluate how their actions will help achieve specified objectives, making them particularly effective for complex tasks requiring planning and foresight.

Core Architecture

Key Components

1. **Goal Formulation Module**

   - Defines explicit objectives
   - Maintains goal hierarchy
   - Updates goals based on context

   Planning System

   - Generates action sequences
   - Evaluates potential outcomes

- Optimizes path to goal

State Monitoring

- Tracks current situation
- Measures progress toward goals
- Detects goal achievement

Practical Examples
1. Navigation System
2. Chess Playing Agent

Real-World Applications
  1. **Industrial Robotics**

Manufacturing robots demonstrate goal-based behavior through:

- Assembly sequence planning
- Quality target achievement
- Resource optimization
- Safety constraint adherence

   Smart Home Systems

Home automation systems utilize goal-based approaches for:

- Temperature management
- Energy optimization
- Security maintenance

4. Lighting control

   Project Management Systems

Project management agents focus on:

- Deadline achievement

- Resource allocation
- Risk minimization
- Budget optimization

Advanced Implementation Patterns
1. Hierarchical Goal Structure
2. Dynamic Goal Adjustment

Performance Considerations

Efficiency Metrics
- Goal achievement rate
- Resource utilization
- Planning time

5. Adaptation speed

Optimization Strategies
1. Goal priority management
2. Resource allocation
3. Plan refinement
4. Performance monitoring

Challenges and Solutions

Common Challenges
1. Goal conflict resolution
2. Resource constraints
3. Environmental uncertainty
4. Real-time planning

Solution Approaches
1. Priority-based goal selection
2. Resource-aware planning
3. Probabilistic goal evaluation
4. Incremental planning

Future Developments of Goal Based Agents

Emerging Trends
1. Integration with machine learning
2. Enhanced goal reasoning
3. Improved planning efficiency
4. Better uncertainty handling

Research Directions
1. Multi-agent goal coordination
2. Advanced goal learning
3. Cognitive architecture integration
4. Real-time replanning.

5. Utility-Based Agents

Utility-based agents go beyond goal achievement by incorporating a utility function, which assigns a numerical value to each possible outcome. They select actions that maximize overall utility, making them ideal for scenarios where multiple solutions exist with varying degrees of desirability.

Core Principles

Utility-based agents utilize sophisticated artificial intelligence that analyses the appealing qualities of different outcomes by employing utility functions. Unlike simpler agent types, these systems can handle many competing goals by assigning numerical values to different states and outcomes.

The concept of utility: The concept of utility plays a vital role and is fundamental to both *economics and computer science*, particularly in the development and creation of utility-based agents. In economics, utility is may be defined as the satisfaction or value gained from through products or services. It is a preference measure, generally expressed as utility functions, that quantifies/measures how much value or happiness a customer obtains from various options.

In computer science, utility-based agents use the concept of utility to make decisions that maximize how well they can achieve goals. Unlike goal-based agents, which focus mainly with completing predetermined goals, utility-based agents evaluate multiple options and select the one that delivers the most utility according to a utility function. These agents utilize sensors to gather data about the environment and actuators to perform actions based on calculated/ estimated utilities. For example, a self-driving car might consider criteria such as safety, speed, and fuel efficiency when selecting the best path. This technique provides for flexibility and adaptability in unknown contexts, making utility-based agents more robust than simpler goal-based agents. *Recall the foundations of AI discussed in chapter 1How various disciplines constitute artificial intelligence.*

Architecture Components

1. **Utility Function**:

- Assigns numerical values to states.

- Represents preferences between states.

   State Evaluation System:

- Analyses the current state in terms of utility.

- Guides the agent in selecting actions that maximize utility.

Decision-Making Process: Utility-Based

The agent performs the following steps:

A. State Perception:

- Observes and interprets the current state of the environment.
- Incorporates different factors into decision-making.

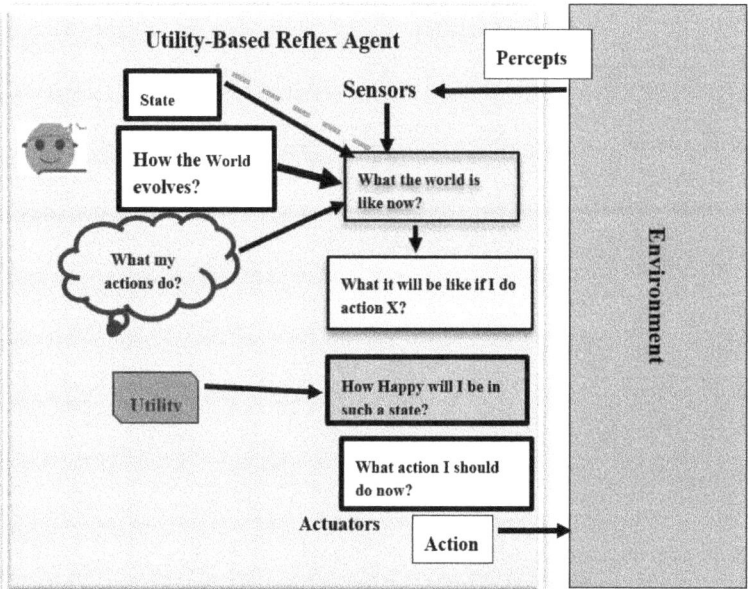

Figure 2.4 Utility-Based Reflex Agent

B. Outcome Prediction:

- Anticipates possible results of actions based on the current state.

C. Utility Calculation:

- Assigns numerical utility values to predicted outcomes using the utility function.

D. Action Selection:

- Chooses the action that maximizes utility based on calculated values.

1. **Implementation Examples:**

Investment Portfolio Manager:

- Analyses market data to evaluate potential investments.
- Predicts outcomes of different investment strategies.
- Maximizes returns by selecting the portfolio with the highest utility value.

Applications:

2. **Healthcare Systems:**

- Medical decision support systems employing utility-based approaches for:
  - Treatment plan optimization
  - Resource allocation
  - Patient scheduling
  - Risk assessment

3. **Energy Management:**

4. **Smart grid systems use utility functions to:**
   - Power distribution
   - Load balance
   - Cost optimization
   - Environmental impact

5. **Financial Trading:**

- **Trading systems with utility-based methods for:**
  - Risk management
  - Portfolio optimization
  - Market timing

- ❖ Asset allocation

Advanced Concepts:

1. **Utility Theory: Multi-Attribute**

2. **Learning Utility Functions:**
   - ❖ Approaches to learning utility functions:
   - ❖ Inverse reinforcement learning
   - ❖ Preference learning
   - ❖ Demonstration-based learning
   - ❖ Experience-based adaptation

3. **Optimization Techniques:**

   - **Utility Function Calibration:**
   - ❖ Parameter improvement
   - ❖ Weight adjustment
   - ❖ Preference alignment

4. **Decision Strategy Optimization:**
   - ❖ Search space pruning
   - ❖ Heuristic approaches
   - ❖ Monte Carlo simulation

4. **Learning Agents:**

Learning agents improve their behaviour over time by learning from past experiences and adapting to new situations. They consist of components like a learning element, performance element, and feedback mechanism, enabling them to evolve in dynamic environments.

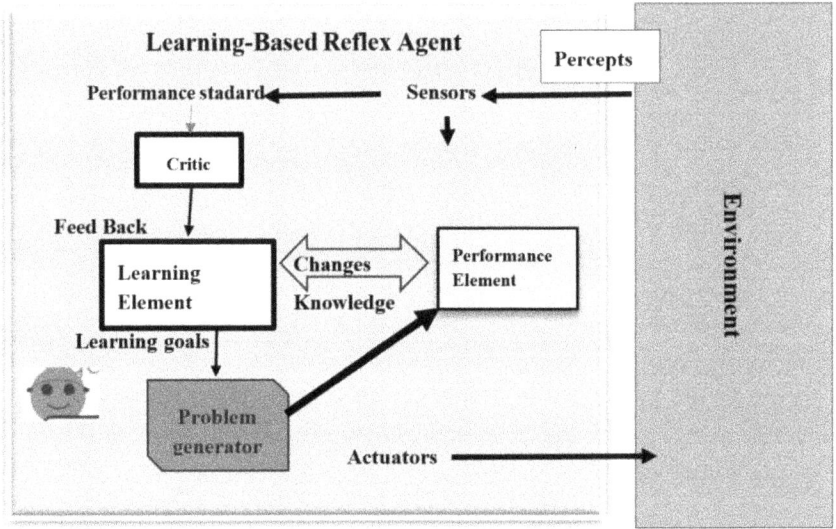

Figure 2.5 Learning Agent

Fundamental Architecture:

Learning agents are the most evolved type of AI agent, distinguished by their capacity to increase performance via experience. The architecture consists of four major components:

1. **Performance Element:**

Selects external actions.
- Responsible for action execution.
- Uses current knowledge in making choices.
- Interfaces with the environment and executes learned policies.
- Learning provides improvements to the knowledge base.
- Modifies behavioral patterns.
- Identifies areas of improvement.
- Processes feedback from the critic
- Updates the decision-making rules.

2. **Critic evaluates the agent's performance.**

   - Provides feedback on actions.
   - generates learning objectives.
   - Monitor progress and identifies areas for improvement.

3. **Problem Generator:**

   - Suggests exploratory acts.
   - creates learning opportunities.
   - Manages the exploration-exploitation trade-off.
   - proposes new scenarios.
   - Tests the agent's capabilities.

Index: Learning Mechanisms

1. **Supervised Learning**

   - Learning from Labelled Examples
   - Pattern recognition
   - Classification tasks
   - Regression issues
   - Direct feedback inclusion

2. **Reinforcement Learning:**

   - Learning through interaction.
   - Reward-Based Feedback
   - Policy Optimization

- Value Function Learning
- **State-action mapping**

3. **Unsupervised Learning**
   - Pattern recognition
   - Clustering
   - Dimensional reduction
   - Feature Learning
   - Structure identification

Applications:

1. **Game Playing**
   - Chess engines
   - Go players
   - Real-time Strategy Games
   - Card game AI and sports simulation

2. **Robotics:**
   - Motion Learning
   - Task Adaptation
   - Environmental interaction
   - Skills: manipulation and navigation.

3. **Natural Language Processing:**
   - Language comprehension Translation systems

- Text generation and sentiment analysis
- Dialogue Systems

Learning Strategies

1. **Online Learning:**
   - Real-time adaptability.
   - Continuous updates
   - Stream processing
   - Incremental learning
   - Dynamic adjustment.

2. **Batch Learning:**
   - Periodic updates.
   - accumulated experience.
   - Stable learning.
   - Comprehensive processing
   - Structured improvement.

3. **Transfer Learning:**
   - Knowledge reuse
   - Domain adaptation
   - Skill transfer
   - Cross-task learning.
   - Experience generalization.

Performance Metrics:

1. **Learning Efficiency:**
   - Learning Rate
   - Convergence Speed
   - Resource utilization
   - Utilization of memory
   - Processing time

2. **Adaptive Capability:**
   - Environmental change reaction
   - Generalization ability
   - Robustness
   - Flexibility
   - Error Recovery

Implementation Considerations:
   - Memory Management
   - Experience storage
   - Information retrieval
   - Memory organization
   - Data prioritization
   - Mechanisms for Forgetting

3. **Exploration Strategies**

    - Random exploration
    - Guided exploration
    - Curiosity-based learning
    - Strategic sampling.
    - Risk assessment

Challenges and Solutions:
    - Common Challenges
    - catastrophic forgetting
    - Sample efficiency
    - Exploration and exploitation balance
    - Real-world deployment
    - Scalability Issues
    - Solutions
    - Continuous learning strategies
    - Experience replay mechanisms.
    - Adaptive exploration methods.
    - Hybrid Architectures
    - Distributed Learning Systems

Future Trends:

1. **Advanced Learning Methods.**
    - Meta-learning abilities.
    - Few-shot learning strategies.
    - Self-supervised learning methods

- Mechanisms allowing continuous adaptation
- Multimodal learning systems

2. **Enhanced Architectures.**
   - Modular Learning Systems
   - Hierarchical learning frameworks/structures
   - Multi-agent learning frameworks.
   - Adaptive neural architectures.
   - Hybrid Learning Models

3. **Application Areas.**
   - Autonomous systems
   - Healthcare Diagnostics
   - Smart Cities
   - Financial systems
   - Environmental monitoring
   - Last revised just now.

5. **Multi-Agent Systems:**

In a multi-agent system, multiple agents interact, either collaboratively or competitively, to achieve individual or shared goals. These systems are common in applications like distributed problem-solving and simulations.

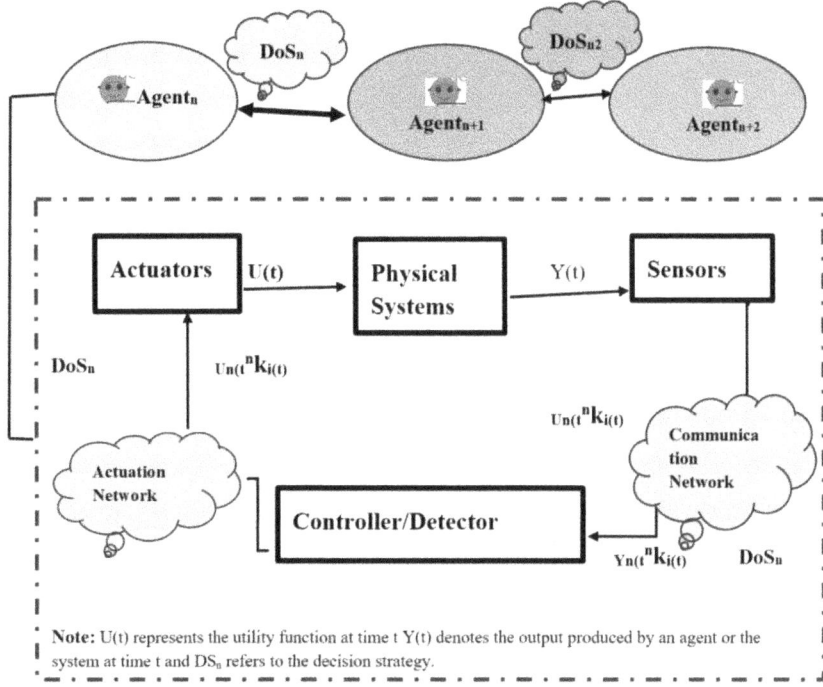

Figure 2.6 Multi-Agent Systems

Fundamental Concepts

Multi-agent systems (MAS) are composed of multiple interacting intelligent agents that collaborate to solve problems beyond their individual capacities. These systems emphasize teamwork and distributed problem-solving methodologies.

Core Characteristics:

1. **Autonomy**

- Independent decision-making.

- Local objective management.

- Self-directed behavior.

   Social Ability:

- Inter-agent communication.

- Negotiation capabilities.
- Coordination protocols.

Reactivity

- Environmental response.
- Adaptive behavior.
- Real-time adjustment.

Proactiveness:

6. **Goal-oriented behaviour.**

   - Taking the initiative.
   - Anticipatory activities.

System Architecture:

1. **Communication Infrastructure**

   - Message-passing protocols.
   - Mechanisms for sharing information.
   - Bandwidth management and network topology.

2. **Coordination Mechanisms:**

   - Task allocation.
   - Resource sharing.
   - Conflict resolution and synchronization methods.

3. **Organization Structures:**

   - Hierarchical.
   - Peer-to-peer networks and hybrid organizations.

- Dynamic reorganization.

4. **Interaction Protocols:**

   - **Cooperation Protocols**
     - Task sharing, result sharing, joint planning, resource allocation.

   - **Negotiation Mechanisms**
     - Bilateral negotiation, Contract Net Protocol, auction procedures, voting schemes.

   - **Conflict Resolution**
     - Arbitration, mediation, voting, priority rules.

Applications:

1. **Distributed Problem Solving:**

   - Search and rescue missions.
   - Traffic management.
   - Power grid management.
   - Supply chain optimization.

2. **Simulation and Modelling:**

   - Social behaviour modelling.
   - Economic systems.
   - Ecological systems.

3. **Urban planning.**

5. **Industrial Applications:**

   - Manufacturing control.
   - Process automation.

- Quality control.
- Logistics management.

Coordination Strategies:

1. **Centralized Coordination**:
   - Central controller.
   - Global optimization.
   - Hierarchical decision-making and resource allocation.

7. **Decentralized Coordination:**
   - Local decision-making.
   - Emergent behavior.
   - Peer interaction.
   - Autonomous adaptation.

8. **Hybrid Approaches:**
   - Mixed-initiative systems.
   - Adaptive organization.
   - Flexible hierarchies.
   - Dynamic reorganization.

Learning in Multi-Agent Systems:
- Collaborative Learning.
- Shared knowledge bases.
- Experience sharing.
- Knowledge synthesis.

6. Competitive Learning:

- Strategic adaptation.
- Game-based learning.
- Adversarial learning.
- Market-based learning.

Performance Considerations:

1. **System Metrics:**
- Scalability.
- Robustness.
- Efficiency.
- Adaptability.

2. **Evaluation Criteria:**
- Task completion rate.
- Resource utilization.
- Communication overhead.
- Response time.

Challenges and Solutions:

1. **Common Challenges:**
- Coordination overhead.
- Communication reliability.
- Scalability issues.

- Resource conflicts.

2. **Solution Approaches:**

- Adaptive coordination mechanisms.
- Reliable communication protocols.
- Hierarchical organization.
- Conflict prevention strategies.

Future Directions:

1. **Advanced Technologies:**

- Blockchain integration.
- AI enhancement.
- Cloud computing.
- Edge computing.

2. **Emerging Applications:**

- Smart cities.
- Autonomous vehicle fleets.
- Environmental monitoring.
- Healthcare systems.

3. **Research Areas:**

- Swarm intelligence.
- Emergent behavior.
- Social learning.
- Trust mechanisms.

Design Considerations:

1. **System Architecture:**
- Scalability planning.
- Fault tolerance.
- Security measures.
- Performance optimization.

2. **Agent Design:**
- Role specification.
- Capability definition.
- Interaction protocols.
- Learning mechanisms.

3. **Environmental Design:**
- Communication infrastructure.
- Resource management.
- Monitoring systems.
- Control mechanisms.

Introduction to Environments in Artificial Intelligence:
In artificial intelligence, an environment is the external context or surroundings in which an intelligent agent acts. Environment-related variables have an important influence/role on agent design, behavior, and performance. Understanding the many types and properties of settings is critical for developing successful AI systems.

AI Environments

AI environments can range from **simple, static** to **sophisticated, dynamic** systems, requiring a variety of agent adaptability. The interaction between the agent and its environment is defined by the agent's perception and actions, which are meant to achieve specific goals. Important factors such as **observability determinism** and the presence of **other agents** all have an important influence on the agent's strategies and algorithms.

The PEAS: Performance, Environment, Actuators, and Sensors) is commonly used for establishing an agent's operational parameters in a structured way, providing clarity in the design and evaluation process.

Table 2.1 Various Environments in AI

Nature of Environment	Description	Examples of PEAS (Performance, Environment, Actuators, Sensors)
Fully Observable	The agent has access to the complete state of the environment at each decision point.	**Performance:** Maximize score in a chess game.
Environment: Chessboard.		
Actuators: Move pieces.		
Sensors: Board configuration.		
Partially Observable	The agent has limited or incomplete information about the environment's state.	**Performance:** Safely navigate a vehicle.
Environment: Road network with traffic.		

Actuators: Steering, accelerator, brakes.		
Sensors: Cameras, LIDAR.		
Deterministic	The next state of the environment is completely determined by the current state and agent's action.	**Performance**: Solve a puzzle efficiently.
Environment: Puzzle board.		
Actuators: Move tiles.		
Sensors: Tile positions.		
Stochastic	The next state of the environment involves randomness or uncertainty.	**Performance**: Maximize points in a dice game.
Environment: Dice and game board.		
Actuators: Roll dice.		
Sensors: Dice results.		
Episodic	The agent's experience is divided into independent episodes, and actions in one episode do not affect others.	**Performance**: Classify images correctly.

Environment: Image dataset.		
Actuators: Label images.		
Sensors: Image pixels.		
Sequential	The current decision could affect future decisions, and actions have long-term consequences.	**Performance**: Win a strategy game.
Environment: Game world.		
Actuators: Perform strategic actions.		
Sensors: Game state.		
Static	The environment does not change while the agent is deciding on an action.	**Performance**: Solve a crossword puzzle.
Environment: Crossword grid.		
Actuators: Fill in words.		
Sensors: Clues and filled cells.		
Dynamic	The environment evolves while the agent deliberates.	**Performance**: Navigate a drone safely.
Environment: Airspace with obstacles.		

Actuators: Adjust altitude and direction.		
Sensors: Proximity sensors, cameras.		
Discrete	The environment has a finite number of distinct states.	**Performance**: Complete a turn-based game.
Environment: Gameboard.		
Actuators: Move pieces.		
Sensors: Game state.		
Continuous	The environment has an infinite number of possible states.	**Performance**: Control a robotic arm.
Environment: Workspace with objects.		
Actuators: Move joints.		
Sensors: Position sensors.		

PEAS (Performance, Environment, Actuators, Sensors)

PEAS is a framework used to define the specific components of an agent's task environment:

1. **Performance Measure**: Defines the success criteria for the agent's operation.
2. **Environment**: Specifies the surroundings or domain in which the agent operates.

3. **Actuators**: Tools or mechanisms through which the agent interacts with its environment.
4. **Sensors**: Devices or methods used to perceive the environment.

Table 2.2 Presents A Summary with G Examples of Environments in AI And the Corresponding PEAS (Performance, Environment, Actuators, Sensors) for agents:

Example Environment	Performance Measure	Environment	Actuators	Sensors
Autonomous Vehicle	Safety, efficiency, speed, passenger comfort	Dynamic, partially observable, stochastic	Steering, throttle, brake, signal lights	Cameras, LIDAR, GPS, speedometer
Chess Playing Agent	Win the game, minimize opponent score	Fully observable, deterministic, discrete	Move pieces on the board	Visual representation of the board
Vacuum Cleaner Agent	Cleanliness of the room, minimal energy usage	Static/dynamic (depending on obstacles), partially observable, deterministic	Motors controlling suction and wheels	Dirt sensors, bump sensors, location sensors
Personal Assistant Agent	Correctness and relevance of responses, user satisfaction	Partially observable, stochastic	Voice responses, text messages	Speech recognition, text input
Robotic Surgery System	Precision, safety, completion of surgical tasks	Static, fully observable, deterministic	Surgical instruments	Cameras, pressure sensors

Stock Trading Agent	Maximize portfolio return, minimize risk	Dynamic, partially observable, stochastic	Buy/sell orders	Market data feeds, historical prices
Search and Rescue Robot	Time efficiency, successful rescue	Dynamic, partially observable, stochastic	Robotic arms, wheels or treads, communication systems	Cameras, infrared sensors, environmental hazard detectors
Smart Thermostat	Maintain desired temperature with minimal energy consumption	Static, fully observable, deterministic	Heating or cooling controls	Temperature sensors, humidity sensors
Traffic Management System	Reduce congestion, optimize traffic flow	Dynamic, partially observable, stochastic	Traffic signals, variable message signs	Traffic cameras, vehicle sensors
E-Commerce Recommendation System	Accuracy and relevance of recommendations, user engagement, conversion rates	Partially observable, stochastic	Display product suggestions	User behavior data, purchase history, browsing patterns

This table is structured with appropriately integrated into the following explanation:

For instance, **Autonomous Vehicle** falls under Dynamic and partially observable Environments.

In the preceding sections of this chapter, we've explored the notion of agents, their classifications, and the many settings in which they work. Agents constitute the foundation of artificial intelligence, representing systems capable of observing their surroundings, making decisions, and performing actions to achieve specific objectives/goals. From simple reflex agents to sophisticated/advanced learning agents, we addressed how these systems interact with and adapt to static and dynamic contexts.

Building on this core concept, the following section (Sections 2.4 and 2.5) explore two major AI applications: chatbots and expert systems. These are specialized agent implementations with the objective to solve real-world communication and decision-making challenges. Chatbots serve as interactive agents enabling human-like communication/interactions on the other hand expert systems simulate the decision-making processes of human experts/professionals in particular subjects.

Together, these concepts provide insights into the practical use of intelligent agents, demonstrating their role in transforming businesses, improving user experiences, and addressing complicated problems.

2.4 Chatbots: Chatbots are software applications created to mimic dialogue with human users, usually via text or voice communication channels. They employ natural language processing (NLP) and machine learning techniques to comprehend user inquiries and produce relevant replies. Basic rule-based chatbots adhere to established conversational frameworks, whereas more sophisticated AI-driven chatbots are capable of managing intricate questions and adapting based on user interactions. These tools are extensively utilized in customer support, information gathering, personal assistance, and entertainment across various websites, messaging services, and voice-activated systems. Their primary benefits include round-the-clock availability, uniform responses, and the capacity to engage in multiple conversations at once.

Figure 2.7 Chatbot (Image generated using Free AI Image Generator: Text to Image Online)

1. **Definition and Purpose**

A chatbot is an **artificial intelligence-powered software application** that simulates conversations or dialogues with human users, typically through text or voice interfaces. Chatbots are widely utilized in client/customer interaction, e-commerce, education, and entertainment.

Types of Chatbots

1. **Rule-Based Chatbots:**

- Follow established rules and scripts.
- Have a limited scope, understanding only specific instructions or inquiries.
- ➢ Example: Automated response systems in customer service.
- ➢ AI-Powered Chatbots:
- Employ natural language processing (NLP) in combination with machine learning.
- Understand context and nuances in language, allowing for more complex interactions.

Examples: ChatGPT, Alexa, and Siri.\

Key Components of Chatbots

1. **Natural Language Processing (NLP):**
   - Enables the bot to interpret and produce human-like text.
2. Includes tasks such as tokenization, sentiment analysis, and intent identification.

Dialogue Management:
Manages the conversation flow, ensuring responses are coherent and contextually appropriate.

3. **Integration APIs:**
   - Connects chatbots to external systems, such as CRM tools or databases, to dynamically retrieve and present information.

Applications

1. **Customer Support:**
   - Provides 24/7 assistance, resolving common queries and directing users to human agents for complex issues.

2. **E-Commerce:**
   - Delivers personalized shopping experiences, product recommendations, and order tracking.

3. **Education:**
   - Facilitates interactive tutoring, language practice, and knowledge sharing.

4. **Healthcare:**
   - Supports symptom checks, appointment scheduling, and health monitoring.

Advantages

1. **Economical and Scalable:**

   - Provides cost-effective solutions, scaling easily to handle increasing user demands.

2. **Availability:**

3. **Offers round-the-clock support to users.**

4. **Personalization:**

   - Enhances user experiences through tailored interactions.

Challenges

1. **Language Comprehension:**

   - Limited in understanding sophisticated language structures.

2. **Training Data:**

   - Relies heavily on the quality of training data for accuracy.

3. **Privacy and Security:**

   - Faces concerns regarding sensitive data handling in private or secure domains.

2.5 Expert Systems: Definition and Purpose

Expert systems are **AI programs** designed to mimic the judgment and decision-making abilities of a **human expert**. They address complex problems by reasoning through information from a specific domain.

2.5.1 Participants in the Development of an Expert System.

The development of an expert system involves the collaboration of three primary participants, each of whom contributes a unique role in assuring the system's success.

Expert.

The expert is a key player whose specialized knowledge creates the base of the expert system. The system's effectiveness depends mainly on the knowledge provided by these domain experts, who have a thorough understanding of the specific topic the system is intended to solve.

Knowledge Engineer.

The knowledge engineer acts as an intermediary between the expert and the system. This individual is responsible for:

Gathering insights from domain experts.

Formalizing and codifying knowledge into the system in a structured manner.

The knowledge engineer verifies that the system's knowledge base is correct, coherent, and relevant to real-world.

End User.

The end-user is the individual or group of people who use the expert system to obtain responses or suggestions for their complex queries. End users might not have domain knowledge expertise, yet they rely on the system's recommendations to make decisions or solve problems. These stakeholders work on the planning, creation, and execution of the expert system, ensuring its effectiveness and relevance for solving domain-specific challenges.

Figure 2.8 Expert Systems (Image generated using Free AI Image Generator: Text to Image Online)

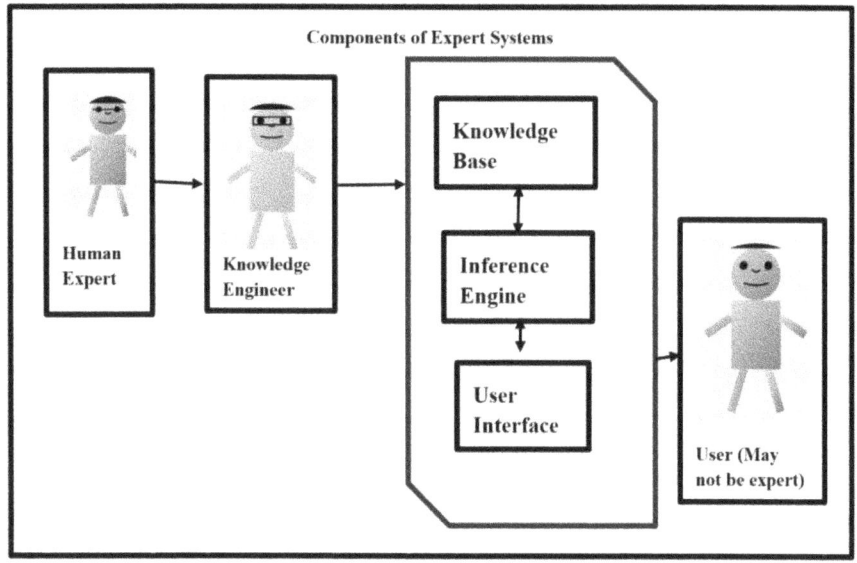

Figure 2.9 Expert Systems

Expert System with Expert Shell System

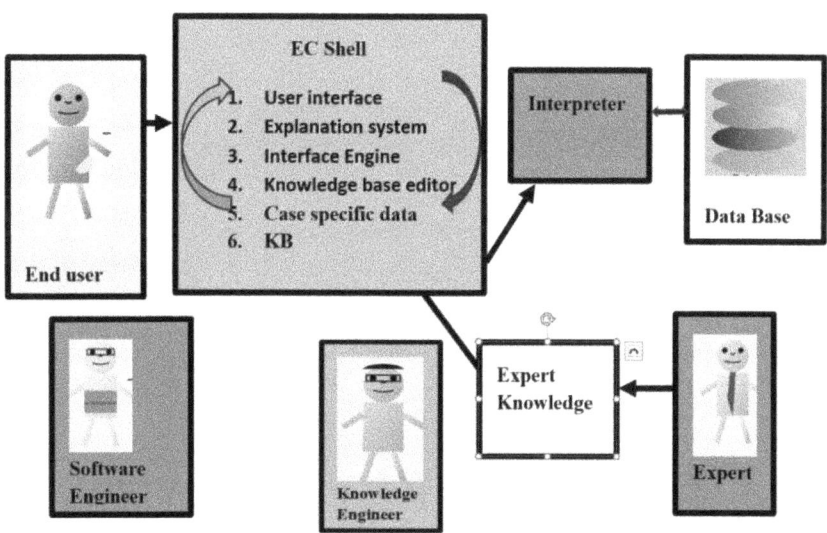

Figure 2.10 Expert Systems with Expert System Shell

Key Characteristics of Expert Systeme:

1. **Knowledge-Based:**

    - Use a knowledge base containing domain-specific facts and rules.

2. **Inference Engine:**

    - A logical reasoning system that applies the knowledge base to draw conclusions or solve problems.

3. **User Interface:**

    - Enables user-system interaction for query input and result output.

4. **Components of Expert Systems Knowledge Base:**

    - Stores both factual and heuristic information about a domain.

    - Typically built with guidance from experts/specialists in the field.

5. **Inference Engine:**

    - Applies rules (e.g., if-then logic) and algorithms to infer new facts from previous data

6. **Explanation Facility:**

    - Provides reasons/explanations for conclusions, enhancing user trust and understanding.

7. **User Interface:**

    - Allows users to send in queries and receive responses or recommendations.

Applications of Expert Systems Medical Diagnosis:

- Systems like MYCIN (for bacterial infections) assist doctors by proposing potential diagnoses and treatment alternatives.

1. **Engineering:**

- Facilitates fault assessment in mechanical systems and network settings.

2. **Finance:**

- **Supports loan approval systems, risk assessment/management, and fraud detection.**

3. **Agriculture:**

- Provides guidance on crop rotation, pest control, and irrigation.

Advantages of Expert Systems:

1. **Consistent Decision-Making:**

- Ensures decisions remain reliable and unbiased.

2. **Data Management:**

Manages vast amounts of data efficiently and effectively.

3. **Reduced Dependence on Human Experts:**

Reduces reliance on experts for repetitive or routine work.

Challenges

1. **Domain Limitation:**

- Restricted to preset/the domains for which ES is made. Lacks the ability to generalize across others domains.

2. **Knowledge Base Quality:**

    - Performance depends mainly on the quality and completeness of the domain knowledge base.

3. **Development Cost and Time:**

    - Building expert systems is often expensive and time-consuming.

Chapter Summary and Concluding Thoughts:

This chapter explored the concept of AI agents, their key traits, and their significance in creating intelligent systems. AI agents are designed to perceive their environment, make decisions, and perform out tasks to achieve specific goals. The discussion focused on the origins and evolution of AI agents, various types/kinds of agents (simple reflex agent, goal-based, utility-based, and learning), and their techniques for gathering and improving on knowledge. The role of multi-agent systems and its potential for dealing with complex, distributed challenges have also been addressed as well as potential future research.

The chapter further addressed design aspects for AI agents, such as the contexts in which they work, which ranged from static to dynamic and completely observable to partially observable. Chatbots, an instance of AI agent, have been discussed, including their different varieties, components, applications, and challenges in disciplines such as customer service and conversational AI. Expert systems, which make assessments using domain-specific knowledge provided by experts in the respecitve fields, were discussed, with an emphasis on components such as the knowledge base, inference engine, and user interface.

AI agents are the foundation for current intelligent systems, with applications in areas as diverse as healthcare, finance, and education. While its benefits include efficiency and scalability, problems such as ethical considerations, robustness, and adaptability nevertheless remain. This chapter sets the foundation for further research into how agents and their components contribute to the broader field of AI and its practical applications.

Chapter – 3
Uncertain Knowledge and Reasoning

Uncertain Knowledge and Reasoning: Quantifying Uncertainty: Acting under Uncertainty, Basic Probability Notation, Inference using Full Joint Distributions, Independence, Baye's Rule and its use.

> AI agent developers rely on probability theory, decision theory, independence assumptions, and Bayes' Rule to quantify and summarize uncertainty. These tools enable the creation of robust programs that reason and act effectively in uncertain environments.

Introduction to Uncertain Knowledge and Reasoning

Uncertainty is an essential feature of real-world decision-making. AI systems often encounter partial/incomplete, unclear, or noisy information/data, making it impossible to operate with entirety certainty. In such situations, reasoning under uncertainty becomes a vital aspect of creating intelligent systems capable of making reasonable choices.

This chapter explores the basic concepts of uncertain knowledge and reasoning, with a focus on how AI systems quantify and manage uncertainty to make good decisions.

Why Uncertainty?
1. Incomplete Knowledge: AI systems frequently lack comprehensive information about the environment they are in.

For example, a medical diagnosis system could not have access to all of the test results required to diagnose a condition.

2. Ambiguity in Observations: Data from sensors or real-world environment might be ambiguous or noisy. A self-driving car, for instance, might fail to comprehend blurry road signals in bad weather.

3. Real-World Systems are complex and dynamic, with various interdependent factors. Creating a deterministic model that encompasses all conceivable situations can often be impractical.

Reasoning Under Uncertainty

To reason under uncertainty, AI systems adopt probabilistic methods to represent and process uncertain knowledge. These methods allow the system to:

- Represent beliefs about unknown variables.

- Update these beliefs dynamically as new evidence becomes available.

- Make decisions that maximize expected utility, even with incomplete information.

Topics in this Chapter

The following key concepts lay the groundwork for reasoning under uncertainty and are elaborated in this chapter:

1. **Quantifying Uncertainty:**

- Discusses how uncertainty can be represented mathematically using probabilities.

2. **Acting Under Uncertainty:**

- Explores decision-making strategies when outcomes are uncertain.

3. **Basic Probability Notation:**

Introduces the fundamental symbols and concepts of probability, such as events, sample spaces, and conditional probabilities.

4. **Inference Using Full Joint Distributions:**
   - Explains how to use joint probability distributions to infer the likelihood of specific events.

5. **Independence:**
   - Highlights the importance of independence assumptions in simplifying probabilistic reasoning.

6. **Bayes' Rule and Its Use:**
   - Demonstrates how Bayes' Rule enables AI systems to update beliefs based on observed evidence.

1. **Quantifying Uncertainty:**

In the real world, decision-making frequently involves incomplete, perplexing or noisy data. Humans regularly encounter unclear/unknown/ situations in which careful judgment is required to make sound decisions. Similarly, AI agents face uncertainty when deciding on the best course of action to attain their objectives or desired outcomes.

Quantifying uncertainty is thus an essential component of developing intelligent systems. Understanding and managing uncertainty helps artificially intelligent devices to make more informed and reliable decisions in complex environments. Uncertainty assessment and quantification are critical in developing robust and adaptive AI systems that can work effectively in the real world. Quantifying the response/action to be taken in uncertainty is a fundamental challenge in decision-making, artificial intelligence, and reasoning systems. This topic encompasses both quantifying uncertainty and the creation of strategies for achieving optimal conclusions in the absence of perfect information.

Uncertainty arises due to the following reasons:

- Incomplete data: Not all relevant information is available.
- Noisy observations can be attributed by measurement or collection errors.
- Inherent randomness: Certain processes inherently stochastic.
- Quantifying uncertainty enables AI and ML tasks to make better choices in such circumstances, enhancing reliability and adaptability.

Types of Uncertainty

Different types of uncertainty must be considered:

- **Aleatory uncertainty**
  - Inherent randomness in a system. The data reveals/displays intrinsic unpredictability.
  - Cannot be reduced, even with infinite data.
  - For example, predicting the outcome of a dice throw or stock market fluctuations.
- **Epistemic uncertainty:** Uncertainty due to limited knowledge. Due to lack of comprehension or information/data/facts.
  - Can be decreased with more data or better modelling strategies.
  - Suppose a model's uncertainty regarding the correct label for a rare class in a classification task.

Model uncertainty: Uncertainty in the mathematical representations used.

Acting Under Uncertainty

When dealing with uncertainty, decision theory gives formal frameworks for making choices. The idea of maximum expected utility implies that rational actors should select activities that maximize their expected utility:

In real-life situations, AI systems must make decisions using insufficient, ambiguous, or noisy information. Acting under uncertainty is the process by which an intelligent agent chooses actions that maximize its chances of reaching/arriving at a desired end, even while it is unable to accurately forecasting the outcomes of those actions.

Why Uncertainty Arises in Decision-Making?

Uncertainty in decision-making stems from various factors:

1. **Incomplete Information**: The agent lacks full knowledge of the environment.

    ❖ Example: A robot navigating a new environment without a complete map.

2. **Noisy Observations**: Data collected by sensors or input devices may be imperfect.

    ❖ Example: A self-driving car misinterpreting blurred road signs due to fog.

3. **Dynamic Environments**: The world changes over time, making predictions difficult.

    ❖ Example: Stock market fluctuations influenced by unforeseen events.

Key Principles of Acting Under Uncertainty

1. **Quantifying Uncertainty**

To act under uncertainty, an agent must first quantify the uncertainty. This is typically done using probability theory, which assigns likelihoods to different outcomes.

- Probability Distribution: A mathematical representation of all possible outcomes and their probabilities.

- Example: Predicting the probability of rain tomorrow based on historical weather data.

2. **Decision Theory**

   Decision-making under uncertainty is guided by **Decision Theory**, which combines probabilities with utilities to evaluate the best course of action.

   > **Decision Theory = Probability Theory + Utility Theory**

   Expected Utility: The agent selects the action that maximizes its expected utility:

   $$EU(A) = \Sigma \, P(O_i|A) \cdot U(O_i)$$

   Where:

   - $EU(A)$: Expected utility of action A.
   - $P(O_i|A)$: Probability of outcome O_i given action A.
   - $U(O_i)$: Utility (value) of outcome O_i.

3. **Trade-offs Between Risk and Reward**

   Agents must balance the potential rewards of an action with the risks associated with uncertainty Risk-Averse and Risk-Tolerant Agents.

   - Risk-Averse Agents: Prefer safer actions with lower variance in outcomes.
   - Risk-Tolerant Agents: opt for actions with higher potential rewards, even if they involve greater risk.
   - Example: A robot choosing between a known, longer path and an unknown, shorter path.

4. **Bayesian Decision-Making**

   Bayesian reasoning helps agents update their beliefs about the environment as new evidence becomes available. This is crucial for refining decisions over time.

   - Example: A medical diagnosis system adjusts the probability of a disease as test results are observed.

Approaches to Acting Under Uncertainty

1. **Probabilistic Models**
   Use probability distributions to model uncertainty in outcomes. Examples include:
   - Bayesian Networks
   - Hidden Markov Models

2. **Reinforcement Learning**
   Agents learn optimal actions by exploring an environment and receiving feedback. This approach is particularly effective in dynamic and uncertain environments.

3. **Heuristic Methods**
   Simplified rules or approximations used when exact calculations are impractical.
   - Example: A chess-playing AI evaluating moves based on experience rather than exhaustively calculating all possibilities.

Summarizing Uncertainty

Uncertainty arises naturally in everyday life due to partial knowledge, complexity, or randomness in data and processes. Understanding and addressing the reasons of uncertainty is crucial in AI and ML as it enables systems to make more informed and logical decisions. This section addresses the primary causes of uncertainty: laziness, theoretical ignorance, and practical ignorance, along with the implications of decision-making.

1. **Laziness:**

Definition: Laziness denotes the difficulty and effort required for building complete rules and models which account for every possible situation/use case.

- Explanation: Creating an exhaustive list of antecedents (conditions) and consequents (outcomes) for every case might not be feasible in some fields of study. Ensuring that rules are exceptionless—valid in all situations—requires significant effort and time.

- Diagnosing diseases is challenging due to patient diversity, making it impossible to list all probable symptoms and their implications.

- Impact on AI: To avoid comprehensive modelling, systems must employ approximate rules or heuristic methods that accept some degree of uncertainty. Probabilistic techniques and machine learning are used to successfully control incompleteness.

2. Theoretical Ignorance:

Definition: Theoretical ignorance arises when there is no complete or commonly accepted theory for a certain subject of knowledge.

Explanation:

- In fields like medicine and study of climate, incomplete comprehension of basic processes can create gaps in theoretical models. The reason why Medical science's incomplete understanding of diseases, like Alzheimer's, necessitates

Impact on AI:
AI systems to rely on partial/incomplete theories and unclear probabilities when predicting outcomes or suggesting treatments.

- AI agents must adapt to uncertainty by using probabilistic reasoning, Bayesian models, or ensemble methods to integrate partial theories and update predictions as new information becomes available.

3. Practical ignorance:

Practical ignorance is the inability to obtain every piece of data needed to make informed choices, regardless of whether a theoretical framework exists.

Explanation

- Practical constraints, such as cost, time, and feasibility, might restrict gathering data.

Example:

A doctor may suspect a medical condition but not be able to confirm it due to high costs or the inadequate availability of tests for diagnosis.

Impact on AI

AI systems use probabilistic methods and inference to fill gaps and forecast outcomes.

Foundations of Probability Theory.

Quantifying uncertainty is often based on probability theory, which provides a mathematical framework for describing and managing uncertain knowledge. This includes: Subjective probability is the representation of the degrees of belief in propositions, which is frequently understood using the Bayesian framework, enabling beliefs to be updated when new evidence becomes available.

4. **Represent Uncertainty:**

The most frequent mathematical framework for expressing uncertainty.
Uses probabilities to describe the likelihood of events or situations.

For example, the weather prediction model could indicate a 70% probability of rain tomorrow.

Bayesian networks:
Directed acyclic graphs showing conditional interdependence between variables. Useful for reasoning in situations that are unclear.

Example: Disease diagnosis based on symptoms.

Fuzzy logic: Deals with thinking that is more approximate than precise. For example, a thermostat may classify a temperature as "warm" with 0.7 certainty and "hot" with 0.3 certainty.

Key Concepts in Probability Theory:

Random Variables

Discrete random variable for example rolling a single die the outcomes that occur(e.g., die rolls) or continuous random variables(height, weight or temperature).

Probability distributions: Define the probabilities associated with different values of a random variable.

Common distributions include Gaussian (Normal), Binomial, and Poisson.

Joint and marginal probabilities:

Joint: The probability of multiple events occurring jointly.

Marginal: The probability of one event regardless of the others.

Conditional probability:

Probability of an event if another event has occurred.

$$P(A|B) = P(A \cap B) / P(B).$$

Bayesian Inference

- **A method of updating beliefs in light of new evidence.**

- **Bayes' Theorem:** Bayes' Theorem is a fundamental principle in probability theory and statistics that describes how to update the probability of a hypothesis based on new evidence.

$$P(H|E) = P(E|H)P(H) / P(E)$$

H: Hypothesis E: Evidence

- $P(H)$ (Prior): The initial probability of the hypothesis before seeing the evidence (your starting belief about H).

- $P(E|H)$ (Likelihood): The probability of observing the evidence E if the hypothesis H is true (how likely the evidence is under the hypothesis).

- P(E) (Marginal Probability): The overall probability of the evidence E, considering all possible hypotheses.

- P(H|E) (Posterior): The updated probability of the hypothesis H after considering the evidence E (your new belief about H).

Decision Theory under Uncertainty

Expected Utility Theory: Expected utility (EU) is a way to measure the value of a decision under uncertainty. It combines the probabilities of different outcomes with their utilities (or "worth") to help us choose the best action. The formula sums up the weighted value of each possible outcome, where the weights are the probabilities of those outcomes given a specific action.

❖ Choose actions that maximize expected utility

$$\text{Expected Utility (EU)} = \Sigma\, P(O_i|A)\, U(O_i)$$

• $P(O_i|A)$: Probability of outcome O_i given action A.

• $U(O_i)$: Utility (value) of outcome O_i.

Risk vs. Reward Trade-off:

❖ Balancing potential rewards against associated risks.

❖ Example: Deciding whether to invest in a high-risk, high-reward stock.

Techniques for Quantifying Uncertainty in ML

A. Ensemble Methods

- Combine predictions from multiple models to estimate uncertainty.

- Examples: Bagging, Boosting.

B. Bayesian Neural Networks

- Incorporate uncertainty in weights by treating them as probability distributions.

C. Monte Carlo Methods

- Use random sampling to approximate probabilities and expectations.

D. Dropout as Bayesian Approximation

- UDropout during inference to estimate model uncertianity

E. Gaussian Process

Provide probabilistic predictions with uncertainty estimates for regression tasks.

Applications of Quantifying Uncertainty

1. Autonomous Systems

- Ensuring safe navigation in unpredictable environments (e.g., self-driving cars).

2. Healthcare

- Diagnosing diseases with confidence scores to aid medical professionals.

3. Finance
- Assessing risk in investment portfolios.

4. Natural Language Processing (NLP)

- Generating confidence scores for predictions in tasks like machine translation or sentiment analysis.

Challenges and Future Directions

Scalability

- Computational cost of representing and propagating uncertainty in large systems.

Interpretability

- Ensuring that uncertainty estimates are understandable to end-users.

Robustness

- Developing systems that remain reliable in high-uncertainty environments.

Ethical Considerations

- Transparent communication of uncertainty to avoid misinterpretation.

Summarizing Uncertainty

Uncertainty is an inherent aspect of real-world environments where AI agents operate. It arises due to factors such as incomplete knowledge, noisy observations, and the inherent randomness of certain events. Quantifying and reasoning about uncertainty allows AI agents to make informed decisions even when the information is ambiguous or incomplete.

In AI, uncertainty is represented and managed using tools like probability theory and Bayes' Rule. These tools enable agents to update their beliefs based on new evidence, infer missing information, and make rational decisions under uncertainty. By leveraging independence assumptions, full joint distributions, and decision theory, engineers can simplify the modelling of uncertainty and design robust systems. This ability to quantify, summarize, and act under uncertainty is critical for applications ranging from autonomous vehicles to medical diagnosis systems.

Basic Probability Notations

Probability theory is a cornerstone of Artificial Intelligence (AI) and Machine Learning (ML), especially when dealing with uncertainty. This section introduces basic probability notations and concepts that form the foundation for understanding probabilistic reasoning, Bayesian inference, and machine learning models.

1. **Sample Space (Ω)**

The **sample space** is the set of all possible outcomes of a random experiment. It is denoted by Ω(Omega)

- Example: In the case of a coin toss, Ω = {Heads, Tails}.
- For rolling a six-sided die, Ω = {1, 2, 3, 4, 5, 6}.

2. **Events (A,B,C,...)**

An **event** is a subset of the sample space, representing a specific outcome or a group of outcomes of interest. Events are typically denoted by capital letters such as A,B,C, etc.

- **Example: For a die roll, the event A (rolling an even number) is A={2,4,6}**
- **Similarly rolling an odd number another event B is B={1,3,7}**

3. **Probability of an Event P(A)**

    The **probability of an event** is a measure of the likelihood of the event occurring. It is denoted by P(A) and satisfies the following properties:

    1. $0 \leq P(A) \leq 1$
    2. $P(\Omega)=1$ (The probability of the entire sample space is 1).
    3. For mutually exclusive events A and B, $P(A \cup B)=P(A)+P(B) = P(A) + P(B)$.

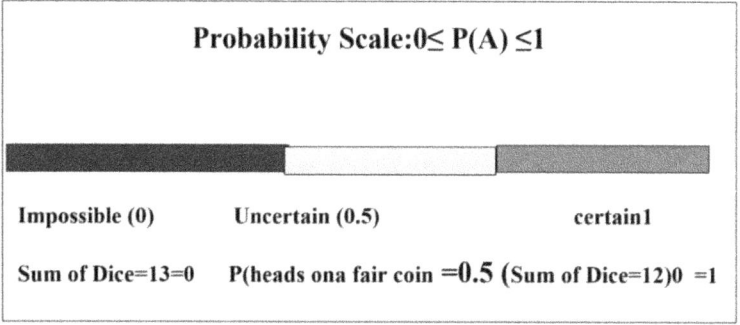

Figure 3.1 Probability of an Event Scale

4. Complement of an Event (A^c)

The **complement** of an event A, denoted A^c (figure 3.2(e)) is the set of outcomes in the sample space that are not in A.

$$P(A^c)=1-P(A)$$

- Example: If A is rolling a 4 on a die, A^c = {1, 2, 3, 5, 6}.

5. Union of Events (A∪B)

The **union** of two events A and B, denoted A∪B (figure 3.2(c)), is the event that either A or B (or both) occur.

$$P(A \cup B) = P(A) + P(B) - P(A \cap B)$$

6. Intersection of Events (A∩B)

The **intersection** of two events A and B, denoted A∩BA (figure 3.2(d)), is the event that both A and B occur simultaneously.

$$P(A \cap B) = P(A) \cdot P(B|A)$$

Where P(B|A)P(B|A)P(B|A) is the conditional probability of B given A.

7. Independent Events

Two events A and B are said to be **independent** if the occurrence of one does not affect the occurrence of the other.

$P(A \cap B) = P(A) \cdot P(B)$

- Example: Tossing two coins: The result of the first coin does not affect the second coin.

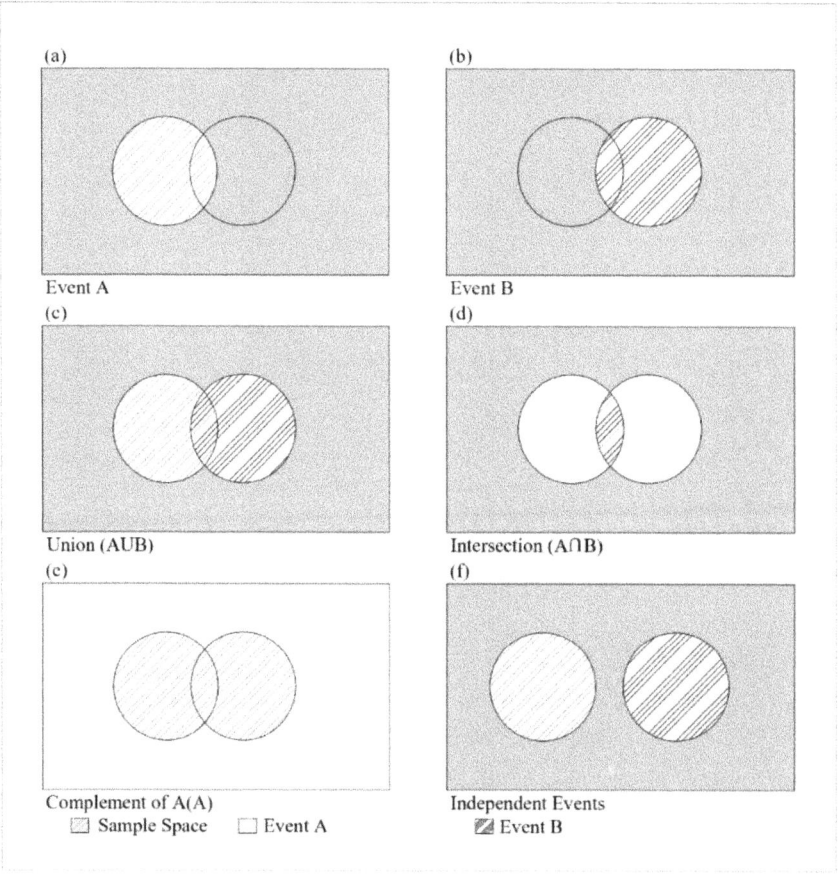

Figure 3.2 Sample space, Events, their complements, unions, intersections, and independent events

8. Conditional Probability (P(B|A)P(B|A)P(B|A))

The **conditional probability** of event B given event A, denoted P(B|A), is the probability that B occurs given that A has occurred.

$$P(B|A) = P(A \cap B) / P(A), P(A) > 0$$

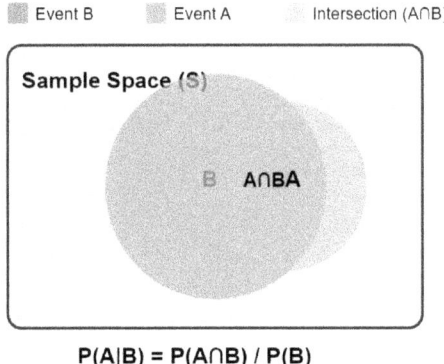

$$P(A|B) = P(A \cap B) / P(B)$$

Figure 3.3 Conditional Probability

9. Inference using Full Joint Distributions:

In probabilistic reasoning, a **full joint distribution** provides a complete description of the probabilities of all possible combinations of variable values in a system. Using this distribution, we can infer the likelihood of specific events or make decisions under uncertainty. However, managing and computing with full joint distributions can be computationally challenging due to their size and complexity.

Full Joint Probability Distribution
A **full joint probability distribution** represents the probability of every possible combination of the values of multiple random variables.

Definition:
Given nn random variables $X_1, X_2, \ldots, X_n$, the full joint distribution is defined as:

$P(X_1, X_2, \ldots, X_n)$

This describes the probability of each possible combination of $X_1, X_2, \ldots, X_n$

Example:
For two binary variables, X (Rain: Yes/No) and Y (Traffic: Heavy/Light), the joint distribution is presented in table 3.1:

Table 3.1 Joint distribution two variables X(Rain) and B(Traffic)

X (Rain)	Y(Traffic)	P(X, Y)
Yes	Heavy	0.3
Yes	Light	0.2
No	Heavy	0.4
No	Light	0.1

Key Concepts in Using Full Joint Distributions

1. Marginalization

Marginalization is the process of summing out one or more variables from the joint distribution to compute the probability of other variables.

Formula:
For two variables X and Y, the marginal probability of X is:

$$P(X) = \sum_{Y} P(X,Y)$$

From the above table:
P(Rain = Yes) = P(Rain = Yes, Traffic = Heavy) + P(Rain = Yes, Traffic = Light) = 0.3 + 0.2 = 0.5

Independence in Relation to Quantifying Uncertainty

Independence is a powerful concept in probability theory that simplifies the representation and computation of joint distributions. When two or more variables are independent, the joint probability distribution of those variables can be factored into smaller, manageable components. This principle is especially useful in AI agent development, where large, complex environments with numerous variables must be modelled efficiently.

By leveraging independence, AI agent developers can reduce computational complexity, making it feasible to reason and make decisions under uncertainty. Below are two examples illustrating how independence simplifies joint distributions in practical scenarios.

Examples of Independence

1. Weather and Dental Problems Are Independent

Scenario:
Suppose an AI healthcare assistant needs to predict the likelihood of a patient having dental problems and bad weather on the same day.

Assumption:
The variables Weather (e.g., W: Rainy or Sunny) and Dental Problems (e.g., D: Present or Absent) are independent because the weather conditions do not influence dental health.

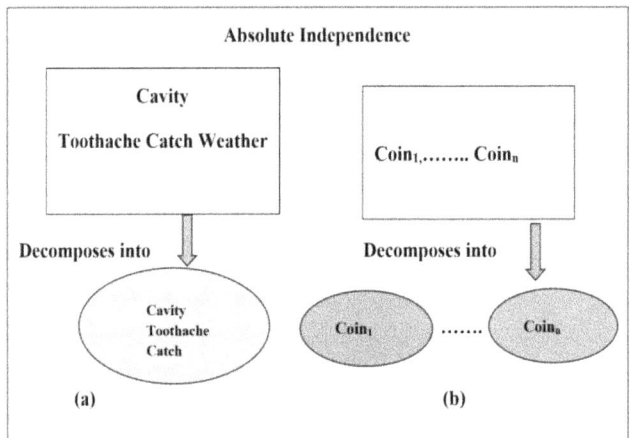

Figure 3.4 Decomposing Joint Probabilities

Two examples of factoring a large joint distribution into smaller distributions, using absolute independence. (a) Weather and dental problems are independent. (b) Coin flips are independent.

Joint Distribution:
If W and D are independent, their joint probability can be factored as:

$$P(W,D)=P(W) \cdot P(D)$$

Simplification:
Instead of calculating and storing probabilities for all combinations of W and D (e.g., Rainy + Present, Rainy + Absent, Sunny + Present, Sunny + Absent), we can store just the marginal probabilities P(W) and P(D).

Implications for AI Agent Development:

- Saves computational resources by reducing the size of the distribution.

- Allows modular reasoning, where weather predictions and dental health predictions can be handled independently.

5. Coin Flips Are Independent

Scenario:
Consider an AI system simulating coin flips to predict outcomes. Let $X_1, X_2, \ldots, X_n$ represent the outcomes of **n** coin flips.

Assumption:
Each coin flip is independent of the others, meaning the outcome of one flip does not influence the outcome of another.

Joint Distribution:
The joint probability of observing a sequence of outcomes X1, X2,...,Xn is the product of the individual probabilities:

$$P(X_1, X_2, \ldots, X_n) = P(X_1) \cdot P(X_2) \cdots \cdots P(X_n)$$

Simplification:
Instead of storing 2^n entries for all possible combinations of outcomes, the system only needs to store the probability of a single coin flip (e.g., P(Heads)=0.5 = 0.5P(Heads)=0.5, P(Tails)=0.5.

Implications for AI Agent Development:

- Facilitates simulations and predictions involving large numbers of coin flips or similar independent events.

- Supports scalability in probabilistic modelling for games, gambling applications, or stochastic simulations.

Role of Independence in AI Agent Development

1. **Efficiency in Computation:** Independence simplifies joint distributions, reducing storage and computational requirements. This is critical for real-time applications where speed and resource efficiency are essential.

2. **Modular Problem-Solving:** Independence allows separate modelling of unrelated variables, enabling modular reasoning. For instance, in multi-agent systems, agents can operate independently unless explicitly coordinated.

3. **Scalability:** Factoring distributions using independence supports scalability, allowing agents to handle large numbers of variables in complex environments.

4. **Improved Decision-Making:** Independence assumptions help focus computational efforts on interdependent variables, improving decision-making efficiency without sacrificing accuracy.

By exploiting independence, AI developers can design agents capable of quantifying uncertainty efficiently. Whether modelling unrelated phenomena like weather and dental health or simulating independent events like coin flips, independence simplifies probabilistic reasoning and enables robust agent design in complex, uncertain environments.

Bayes' Theorem: Theorem is central to probabilistic reasoning in artificial intelligence. It enables agents to adapt, learn, and make informed decisions in difficult contexts, making it critical for creating robust and intelligent systems. Understanding and properly implementing Bayes' Theorem is critical for the advancement of artificial intelligence.

Bayes' Theorem relates conditional probabilities and is a fundamental concept in probabilistic reasoning.

$$P(A|B) = P(B|A) \cdot P(A) / P(B), P(B) > 0$$

- P(A|B): Probability of A given B.
- P(B|A): Probability of B given A.
- P(A): Prior probability of A.
- P(B): Marginal probability of B.

Importance of Bayes' Theorem in AI Agent Design:

Bayes' Theorem is essential for the design and functionality of AI agents since it allows for probabilistic reasoning, decision-making under uncertainty, and data-driven learning. That's how it contributes:

Handling/Addressing Uncertainty AI agents often operate in environments where information/data can be partial/incomplete, noisy, or confusing/ambiguous. Bayes' Theorem provides a mathematical framework for revising an agent's beliefs about the world based on observed data.

For instance, a self-driving car that detects a pedestrian in low-visibility circumstances may employ Bayesian inference to determine the likelihood of a pedestrian's presence based on sensor data.

- **Probabilistic reasoning:**

Bayesian reasoning permits artificially intelligent devices to make informed judgments/decisions through the combination of prior knowledge (beliefs) with new data. As is the case in medical diagnosis systems, the agent updates the likelihood of a disease based on apparent symptoms and prior disease probabilities

- **Decision-Making with Uncertainty:**

Bayes' Theorem is used in decision-making frameworks such as Bayesian Decision Theory, in which an AI agent evaluates the best course of action according to probability and potential outcomes.

Another instance such as, in a robot navigation system, the agent relies on Bayesian reasoning to figure out the safest path by evaluating the possibility of obstacles across different routes.

- **Establishing and Updating Beliefs** Bayesian methods enable AI agents to learn from data by iteratively updating their beliefs. This is especially beneficial in dynamic settings where conditions vary over time. In the case of a recommendation system can update its understanding of user preferences in response to new user interactions.

- **Building Robust Models:** Bayes' Theorem is vital for creating models like: Naive Bayes Classifiers are simple but effective for classification problems.

  Bayesian networks represent intricate probabilistic relationships among variables. These models are used in an extensive variety of AI applications, such spam detection and risk assessment.

- **AI Subfield Applications: Bayes'** Theorem has been utilized in several AI domains: Natural Language Processing (NLP) involves calculating word probabilities in text classification. Computer vision is a method of inferring the presence of objects from ambiguous/ confusing visual data.

  Robotics: Simultaneous Localization and Mapping (SLAM), whereby a robot maps the environment while positioning itself inside them.

Enabling Explainability: Bayes' Theorem: Bayesian reasoning offers a probabilistic basis for AI agent decisions, rendering them more understandable.

In essential applications such as healthcare, an AI agent can apply Bayes' Theorem to demonstrate how evidence contributes to a specific diagnosis.

Chapter Summary and Concluding Thoughts

In this chapter explored into the fundamental concepts of reasoning under uncertainty, that are a vital component for creating strong/ robust AI agents. are studied the importance of probability theory, decision theory, and independence assumptions in assessing and handling uncertainty in dynamic environments. The primary topics included employing basic probability notation to represent uncertain instances, using Bayes' Rule to modify/alter beliefs with updated information/data, and building entirety joint distributions to infer probabilities. The chapter also looked at how these tools let AI systems perform rationally in an environment of uncertainty, employing decision-making frameworks to maximize expected utility while balancing risks and rewards.

Uncertainty is inherent in real-world decision-making, and the ability to reason effectively in such circumstances is critical to AI. Artificial intelligence bots may employ probabilistic techniques to navigate incomplete or noisy input and make intelligent decisions. This chapter emphasized the way comprehending concepts like Bayes' Rule, independence, and joint distributions helps developers to develop intelligent systems that can adapt to a variety of unanticipated events.

Chapter - 4
Search and Search Strategies

Search and search strategies- Problem-solving agents, Example problems, Searching for Solutions Uninformed Search Strategies: Breadth First search, Depth First Search, Iterative deepening depth first search. Informed Search Strategies: Heuristic functions, Greedy best first search, A*search. Logical Agents.

> "Search strategies are fundamental tools for problem-solving agents in Artificial Intelligence, enabling them to navigate complex decision-making scenarios and find solutions in problem spaces using both uninformed and informed approaches their applications in solving real-world problems."

Search is an essential concept in Artificial Intelligence (AI), laying the foundation for strategies for solving problems required to navigate complex decision-making environments. It comprises specifically exploring a variety of different states or configurations with the aim achieve a specific objective/goal. Search algorithms provide the structure for tackling a number of challenges, such finding the shortest path in a network, solving puzzles, and planning activities. This chapter covers some search strategies, both uninformed and informed, and illustrates how AI systems employ these approaches to identify efficient solutions. Presented are the principles that allow AI to reason, plan, and act effectively in a broad spectrum of problem domains through real-world examples and clear explanations.

Problem Solving Agents

Problem-solving agents are systems which meticulously evaluate possible actions and states for solving complex problems. These agents employ structured strategies like search algorithms, heuristics, and methods of optimization to accomplish their goals. Examples of route planning agents in navigation systems and puzzle-solving agents in games demonstrate how these agents operate in real-world and abstract domains, respectively. By utilizing suitable search strategies, these agents can efficiently find optimal or near-optimal solutions to challenging problems.

Key Characteristics of Problem-Solving Agents:
1. **Goal-Driven Behaviour**: Problem-solving agents are driven by specific goals, navigating a defined state space to achieve desired outcomes.
2. **State Space Representation**: Problems are modelled as states and actions, where each state represents a configuration of the environment, and actions define transitions between states.
3. **Search Strategies**: Agents employ to explore the state space. These can be:
   - Uninformed Search: Lacking additional information about the goal.
   - Informed Search: Guided by to improve efficiency.

Operating Process of Problem-Solving Agents

Problem-solving agents employ a structured method to solve problems.
1. Define the goal: Identify the desired outcome.
2. Represent the problem as states, actions, and limitations.
3. To seek a solution, use to identify a number of actions which contribute to the intended result.

4. Implement the Solution: Use the given solution to achieve the goal.

Components of a Problem-Solving Agent

To operate effectively, problem-solving agents rely on the following components:

To operate effectively, problem-solving agents rely on the following components:

- State Space Representation: A model of all possible states and actions in the environment.
- Initial State: The starting configuration of the problem.
- Goal Test: A condition to determine if the goal state is reached.
- Action Set: The set of possible actions available to the agent.
- Transition Model: Rules that define how actions transform states.
- Path Cost Function: A measure of the cost associated with a sequence of Path Cost.

By combining these characteristics and components, problem-solving agents systematically explore their environment to identify and execute solutions, making them essential tools in for addressing a wide range of decision-making and planning tasks.

Types of Search Algorithms:

Search algorithms can be broadly classified into two categories based on their approach and the information they use to navigate the problem space. Figure 3.1 presents types of algorithms in AI

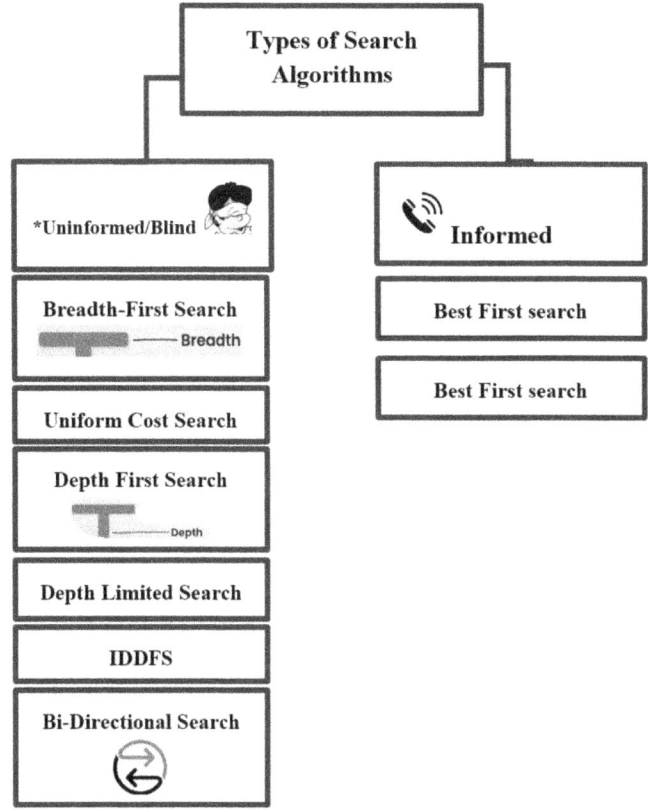

Figure 4.1 Types of Search Algorithms in AI

1. **Uninformed Search Algorithms:**

    - Definition: Also known as blind search, these algorithms have no additional information about the goal state beyond the problem definition.

---

[1] https://www.dreamstime.com/royalty-free-stock-photo-cartoon-man-blindfold-image21213705 for blindfold cartoon icon webpage And https://www.vectorstock.com/royalty-free-vector/call-icon-noisy-phone-flat-calling-symbol-vector-33282617 We gratefully acknowledge the use of two icons only in this page ok?

[2] https://www.dreamstime.com/royalty-free-stock-photo-cartoon-man-blindfold-image21213705 for blindfold cartoon icon webpage And https://www.vectorstock.com/royalty-free-vector/call-icon-noisy-phone-flat-calling-symbol-vector-33282617 We gratefully acknowledge the use of two icons

- Examples:
  - ❖ **Breadth-First Search (BFS):** Explores all nodes level by level; complete and optimal for uniform cost.
  - ❖ **Depth-First Search (DFS)** Explores as deep as possible before backtracking; not guaranteed to be optimal.
  - ❖ **Iterative Deepening Depth-First Search (IDDFS)** Combines BFS and DFS to balance completeness and memory efficiency.
- Advantages: Simple implementation; guarantees completeness for BFS and IDDFS.
- Disadvantages: Inefficient for large or infinite state spaces.
- **Informed Search Algorithms**
- **Definition:** These algorithms use heuristic functions to guide the search process toward the goal more efficiently.
- **Examples:**
  - ❖ **Greedy Best-First Search (GBFS)** Prioritizes nodes with the lowest heuristic cost; faster but not optimal.
  - ❖ **A* Search Algorithm** Combines path cost and heuristic cost $f(n)=g(n)+h(n)$ to find the optimal solution.
- **Advantages:** More efficient for large state spaces; optimal with appropriate heuristics.
- **Disadvantages:** Performance heavily depends on the quality of the heuristic.

Understanding these properties and types helps in selecting the most suitable algorithm for solving different problems in AI.

Essential Properties of Search Algorithms:
Search algorithms, a cornerstone of are evaluated based on several essential properties that determine their efficiency and applicability to various problems. These properties help in understanding the trade-offs

involved in choosing an algorithm for solving a specific problem. The four essential properties of search algorithms are:

1. **Completeness:**

    - **Definition:** A search algorithm is complete if it guarantees finding a solution, provided one exists.

    - **Importance:** Completeness ensures reliability, especially in critical applications where finding a solution is mandatory.

    - **Example**: BFS is complete because it systematically explores all possible states.

    - **Limitations**: Algorithms like DFS may fail to be complete in infinite or cyclic state spaces unless enhanced with cycle detection.

2. **Optimality**

    - **Definition:** An algorithm is optimal if it guarantees finding the best solution, typically the one with the least cost.

    - **Importance:** Optimality is crucial in applications where cost minimization (e.g., shortest path or least resource usage) is required.

    - **Example:** A* search algorithm is optimal when using an admissible heuristic.

    - **Limitations:** Greedy Best-First Search is not optimal as it prioritizes heuristic estimates over path cost.

3. **Time Complexity**

    - **Definition:** The time complexity of an algorithm measures the number of nodes it explores to find a solution.

    - **Importance:** Algorithms with lower time complexity are desirable for problems with large state spaces.

- **Example: Iterative** Deepening Depth-First Search (IDDFS) combines the benefits of BFS and DFS, offering efficient time complexity for deep problems.

- **Limitations:** Limitations of BFS has high time complexity for problems with deep solutions, as it explores all nodes at each level.

4. **Space Complexity**
   - **Definition**: Space complexity refers to the amount of memory required by an algorithm during execution.
   - **Importance**: Memory-efficient algorithms are essential for handling large problems with constrained computational resources.
   - **Example**: DFS has low space complexity since it only needs to store a single path from the root to the current node.
   - **Limitations**: BFS requires storing all nodes at the current level, leading to high space complexity.

Breadth-First Search (BFS)

Breadth-First Search (BFS) is one of the fundamental uninformed search strategies in artificial intelligence. It systematically expands and examines all nodes of a tree or graph structure by exploring all neighbour nodes at the present depth before moving to nodes at the next depth level.

Description of BFS Algorithm

BFS works by following these steps:
1. Start at the root node and add it to a queue
2. Remove the first node from the queue and examine it
3. Add all unvisited neighbor nodes to the queue
4. Repeat steps 2-3 until the queue is empty or goal is found

BFS algorithm uses a First-In-First-Out (FIFO) queue data structure to maintain the frontier of nodes to be explored,

Properties of BFS
1. **Completeness:** BFS is complete, meaning it will always find a solution if one exists in a finite state space.
2. **Optimality:** When path costs are uniform, BFS is optimal as it finds the shallowest goal node first.
3. **Time Complexity:** $O(b^d)$, where b is the branching factor and d is the depth of the solution.
4. **Space Complexity:** $O(b^d)$, as it needs to store all nodes at the current level.

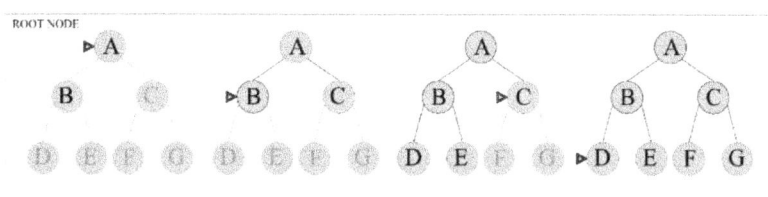

Figure 4.2 Breadth-First Search

Disadvantages:
1. Memory intensive due to storing all nodes at current level
2. May be slow for very deep solutions
3. Not suitable for infinite state spaces

Applications:
1. Shortest path finding in unweighted graphs
2. Web crawling
3. Social network friend suggestions
4. GPS navigation systems
5. Puzzle solving

Depth-First Search (DFS)
Depth-First Search (DFS) is a prominent uninformed search technique used in AI and computer science. It investigates a problem space by going as far as possible down one branch before returning to examine other

branches. DFS is particularly useful in cases where the search space is large and memory efficiency is crucial.

How DFS Works?

DFS starts at the initial state (or root node) and explores a path by visiting the deepest unvisited node first. If it reaches a dead end (i.e., a state with no further unvisited neighbors or where all paths have been explored), it backtracks to the previous node and explores alternative paths.

Algorithm Steps

1. **Initialization**: Start at the initial state and push it onto a stack.

2. **Exploration**:

    ❖ Pop the top node from the stack.

    ❖ Check if it is the goal state. If yes, terminate and return the solution.

    ❖ If not, expand the node and push its unvisited neighbors onto the stack.

3. **Backtracking**: Repeat the process until the stack is empty or the goal is found.

4. **Termination**: If the stack is empty and no solution is found, conclude that no solution exists.

DFS can be implemented using a stack (explicitly or via recursion). The recursive implementation is often simpler but may lead to stack overflow for very deep search spaces.

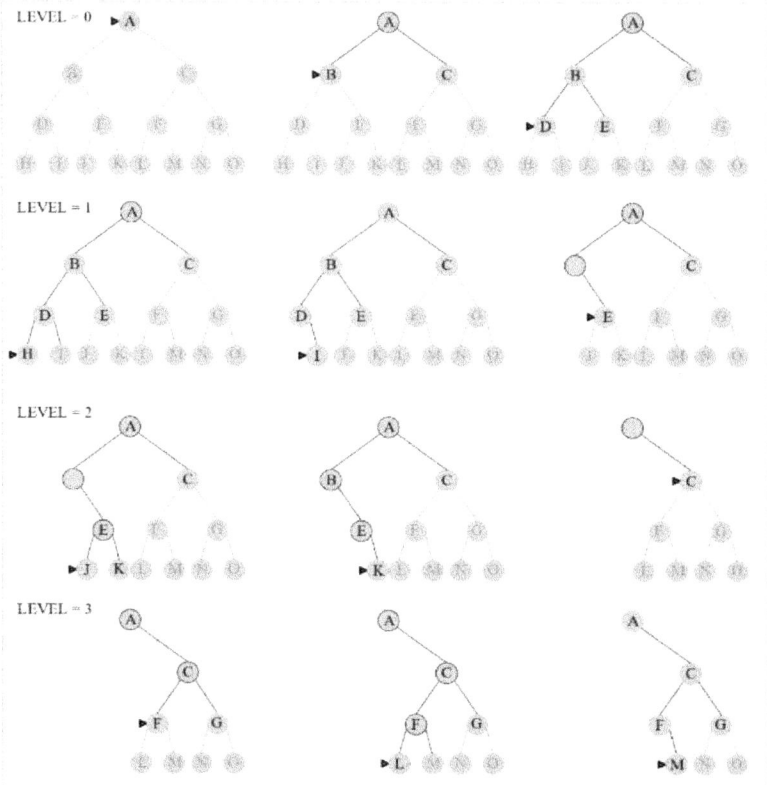

Figure 4.3 Depth First Search

Example: Solving a Maze with DFS

Consider traversing a maze. Starting at the entrance, DFS follows a single path until it reaches either the exit (target state) or a dead end. Whenever it hits a dead end, it reverses around and takes a different path. This process repeats until the exit is found or all paths have been explored.

Advantages of DFS

1. **Memory Efficiency:**

    - DFS uses memory proportional to the depth of the deepest branch being explored ($O(d)$.[unlike Breadth-First Search (BFS), which requires storing all nodes at a level ($O(b^d)$)].

- Ideal for problems with large state spaces and limited memory resources.

2. **Suitable for Deep Solutions:**

   ➤ If the solution lies deep in the state space and paths are narrow, DFS can be more efficient than BFS.

3. **Easy to Implement:**

DFS can be implemented using either recursion or an explicit stack, making it straightforward to code.

Disadvantages of DFS

1. **Non-Optimal:**

   - DFS does not guarantee finding the shortest or least-cost solution.
   - It may explore unnecessarily deep branches, ignoring closer solutions.

4. **Completeness:**

   - DFS is not complete in infinite or cyclic state spaces unless additional mechanisms (e.g., cycle detection) are employed.

5. **Susceptible to Getting Stuck:**

   - In state spaces with infinite depth or large branching factors, DFS can get stuck exploring infinite or unproductive paths.

Applications of DFS
DFS is used in various domains where memory efficiency is critical, and a solution doesn't necessarily have to be optimal. Examples include:

1. **Game Tree Exploration**: DFS is employed in exploring possible moves in games like chess.
2. **Pathfinding in Mazes**: Used to find a path between points in a maze or grid.

3. **Topology and Graph Algorithms**:
   - **Connected Components**: Finding connected components in a graph.
   - **Topological Sorting**: Ordering nodes in a directed acyclic graph.

Variants of DFS

6. **Iterative Deepening Depth-First Search (IDDFS)**:
   - Combines the space efficiency of DFS with the completeness and optimality of BFS.
   - Explores the search space iteratively with increasing depth limits.

- **Bidirectional DFS:**
  - Searches simultaneously from the initial state and the goal state, meeting in the middle.

DFS is an effective tool in the AI toolbox, especially when memory efficiency and deep search capabilities are essential. However, its limitations are in fulfilling optimality and completeness requirements. These aspects must be addressed through modifications or by combining it with other search algorithms.

Depth-Limited Search (DLS)

Depth-Limited Search (DLS) is a variation of Depth-First Search (DFS) that introduces a predetermined depth limit to prevent the search from descending indefinitely into deep or infinite state spaces. It is particularly useful when the search space is large or potentially unbounded, and there is a need to control resource consumption, such as memory and computation time.

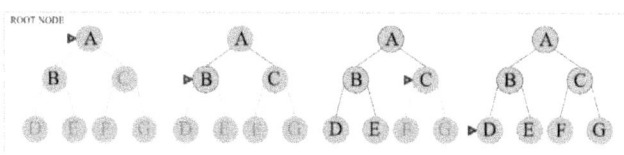

Figure 4.4 Depth-Limited Search.

Key Features of Depth-Limited Search

1. **Depth Restriction:**
   DLS adds a maximum depth, lll, which limits the search to nodes within lll levels of the initial state. Nodes beyond this depth are not expanded.

2. **Avoidance of Infinite Loops:**
   By imposing a depth limit, DLS eliminates the risk of getting trapped in cycles or infinite paths that might occur in some state spaces.

Advantages of Depth-Limited Search:

- Memory Efficiency: Like DFS, it uses a stack-based approach and requires less memory compared to breadth-first search.

- Control Over Search Depth: Prevents unnecessary exploration of irrelevant deep paths.

- Applicable for Infinite State Spaces: Can explore parts of infinite state spaces without running indefinitely.

Limitations of Depth-Limited Search:

- Incomplete Search: DLS may fail to find a solution if the solution lies beyond the specified depth limit.

- Non-Optimal Solutions: It does not guarantee the shortest or most cost-effective path to the goal.

- Choice of Depth Limit: Choosing an appropriate depth limit can be challenging. If the limit is too small, the solution might be missed; if too large, resource consumption increases unnecessarily.

Applications of Depth-Limited Search:

- Suitable for domains with very deep or infinite state spaces where resource constraints need to be managed.

- Often used as a foundational concept for iterative deepening search (IDDFS Iterative Deepening Depth-First Search.

Table 4.1 Comparison to Depth-First Search with Depth Limited Search

Feature	Depth-First Search (DFS)	Depth-Limited Search (DLS)
Exploration Depth	Unlimited, may go infinitely deep	Restricted to a predefined depth lll
Completeness	Not guaranteed in infinite state spaces	Depends on depth limit lll
Optimality	Not optimal	Not optimal
Memory Usage	Low, proportional to the depth of the tree	Low, similar to DFS

Depth-Limited Search strikes a balance between resource efficiency and the need to control exploration depth, making it a valuable technique in specific problem-solving scenarios.

Iterative Deepening Depth-First Search (IDDFS)
Iterative Deepening Depth-First Search (IDDFS) is a hybrid algorithm that combines the memory efficiency of Depth-First Search (DFS) with the completeness and optimality of Breadth-First Search (BFS). It is particularly useful for problems with large or infinite state spaces where the depth of the solution is unknown.

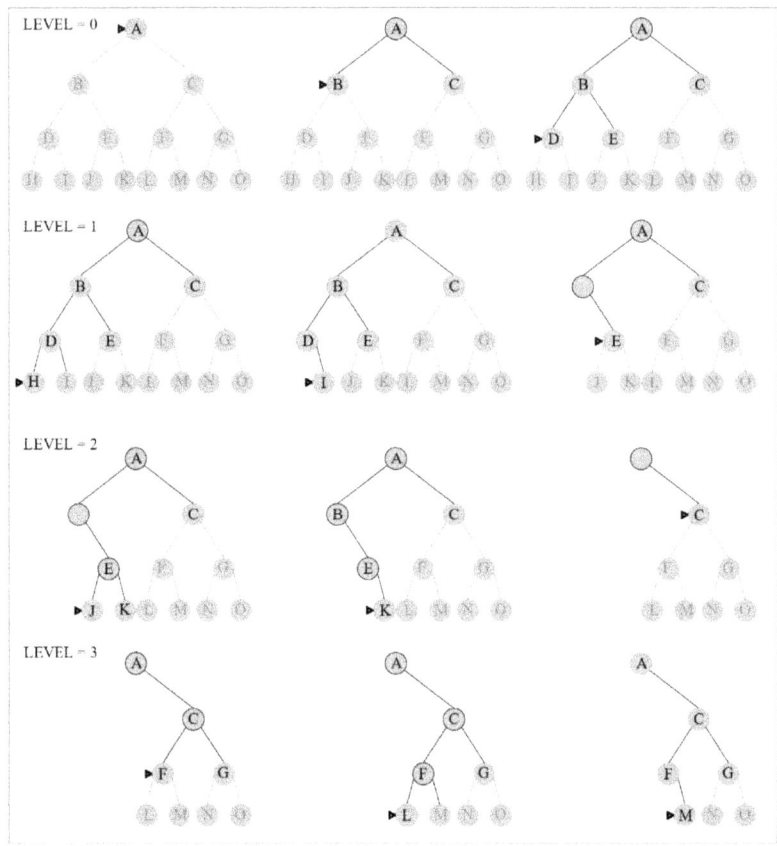

Figure 4.5 Iterative Deepening Depth-First Search (IDDFS)

How IDDFS Works?

IDDFS performs a series of depth-limited searches, incrementally increasing the depth limit until a solution is found. At each iteration, it explores nodes up to the current depth limit using DFS, restarting from the root node for the next deeper limit.

Algorithm Steps

1. **Initialization:**
    - Start at the initial state and set the depth limit to 0.

2. **Depth-Limited Search:**
    - Perform a DFS with the current depth limit.

- If a solution is found, terminate and return the solution.
- If no solution is found, increase the depth limit and restart the search.

3. **Iteration:**
   - Repeat the process until the solution is found or all possible states are explored.

Example of IDDFS

Consider finding a solution in a simple tree structure:

1. **Depth Limit = 0**: Explore only the root node.
2. **Depth Limit = 1**: Explore all nodes at depth 1 (children of the root).
3. **Depth Limit = 2**: Explore all nodes at depth 2 (grandchildren of the root).
4. Continue this process until the goal node is found.

Advantages of IDDFS

1. **Completeness:**
   - IDDFS is complete, ensuring that a solution will be found if one exists, even in infinite state spaces.

2. **Optimality:**
   - Like BFS, IDDFS finds the optimal solution (in terms of the shortest path) in uniform-cost search scenarios.

3. **Memory Efficiency:**
   - IDDFS uses memory proportional to the depth of the current search ($O(d)$), similar to DFS, making it far more space-efficient than BFS ($O(b^d)$).

4. **Balanced Approach:**

    - Combines the systematic exploration of BFS with the low memory requirements of DFS.

Disadvantages of IDDFS

1. **Repeated Exploration:**

    - Nodes near the root are explored multiple times across iterations, leading to redundant computations. However, this overhead is often manageable compared to BFS's memory requirements.

2. **Time Complexity:**

    - Although the asymptotic time complexity is $O(bd)O(b^d)O(bd)$, the repeated exploration can slightly increase actual runtime compared to BFS.

Applications of IDDFS

1. **Pathfinding in Graphs:**

    - IDDFS is widely used in large graphs or trees where the solution depth is unknown.

2. **Game Trees:**

    - In game tree exploration, IDDFS helps find solutions in games like chess, where the depth of the solution may vary.

3. **Artificial Intelligence (AI):**

    - Used in AI systems to search through state spaces efficiently with limited memory resources.

4. **Robotics:**

    - IDDFS is employed in navigation systems where both completeness and memory efficiency are critical.

Table 4.2 Comparison of IDDFS with Other Algorithms

Aspect	IDDFS	DFS	BFS
Completeness	Guaranteed	Not guaranteed in infinite spaces	Guaranteed
Optimality	Guaranteed for uniform-cost problems	Not guaranteed	Guaranteed for uniform-cost problems
Memory Efficiency	$O(d)$	$O(d)$	$O(b^d)$
Time Complexity	$O(b^d)$	$O(b^d)$	$O(b^d)$

IDDFS is a versatile algorithm that strikes a balance between memory efficiency and solution completeness, making it highly effective for AI and graph-related problems.

Bidirectional Depth-First Search (Bidirectional DFS)

Bidirectional DFS is an optimization of the standard Depth-First Search (DFS) algorithm that simultaneously searches from both the start state and the goal state. The two searches proceed in opposite directions, and the algorithm terminates when they meet at a common node. This approach reduces the search space significantly, making it faster for many problems.

How Bidirectional DFS Works?

The idea behind Bidirectional DFS is to split the search into two parts:

1. One search begins from the **start node** and explores towards the goal.
2. The other search starts at the **goal node** and explores backwards towards the start node (requires knowledge of reverse transitions).

The search alternates between the two directions and stops when a node is visited by both searches, indicating a path exists between the start and goal nodes.

Algorithm Steps

1. **Initialization:**

   - Create two stacks: one for the forward search and one for the backward search.

   - Add the start node to the forward stack and the goal node to the backward stack.

2. **Alternate Searches:**

   - Perform a depth-limited DFS from the forward stack.

   - Perform a depth-limited DFS from the backward stack.

3. **Check Intersection:**

   - After each step, check if any node has been visited by both searches. If so, a solution is found.

4. **Termination:**

   - If no solution is found and both stacks are empty, conclude that no path exists.

Advantages of Bidirectional DFS

1. **Reduced Search Space:**

   - Bidirectional search reduces the effective depth of the search space. Instead of exploring $O(b^d)$ where b is the branching factor and d is the depth, it explores approximately $O(b^{d/2})$ in each direction.

2. **Memory Efficiency:**

   - Like standard DFS, it requires memory proportional to the depth of the search (O(d)) rather than the size of the state space.

3. **Faster Search:**

   - By halving the depth to be explored, Bidirectional DFS finds solutions more quickly than a single-direction DFS in many cases.

Disadvantages of Bidirectional DFS

1. **Requires Reverse Transitions:**

   - For the backward search, the algorithm must know how to reverse actions or transitions, which may not always be possible.

2. **Synchronization Overhead:**

   - Managing and synchronizing two separate DFS processes can be complex.

3. **Non-Optimal Solutions:**

   - Like standard DFS, Bidirectional DFS does not guarantee finding the shortest or least-cost path unless further optimization is applied.

Applications of Bidirectional DFS

1. **Pathfinding:**

   - Used in navigation and graph traversal problems where both the start and goal nodes are known.

2. **Game Trees:**

   - Applied in games like chess or checkers to find moves leading to a desired state.

3. **Network Routing:**

    - Useful in routing algorithms to find a connection between two nodes in a network.

Table 4.3 Comparison of Bidirectional DFS with Other Algorithms

Aspect	Bidirectional DFS	DFS	BFS
Search Space	$O(b^{d/2})$	$O(b^d)$	$O(b^d)$
Memory Efficiency	$O(d)$	$O(d)$	$O(b^d)$
Optimality	Not guaranteed	Not guaranteed	Guaranteed for uniform-cost problems
Completeness	Guaranteed if no infinite paths exist	Not guaranteed in infinite spaces	Guaranteed

Example Use Case

Problem: Finding the shortest route between two cities.

- Forward Search: Starts from City A and explores roads towards City B.

- Backward Search: Starts from City B and explores roads towards City A.

- The search ends when both searches meet at a common city, indicating a connection between City A and City B.

Bidirectional DFS is a powerful extension of standard DFS, particularly in scenarios where reducing the search space is critical. However, its effectiveness depends on the ability to implement reverse transitions and manage two simultaneous search processes efficiently.

Greedy Best-First Search (GBFS):

Greedy Best-First Search is an that prioritizes exploration of nodes based on a heuristic function. Unlike uninformed search algorithms, GBFS uses domain-specific knowledge to make decisions, aiming to move toward the goal state as quickly as possible.

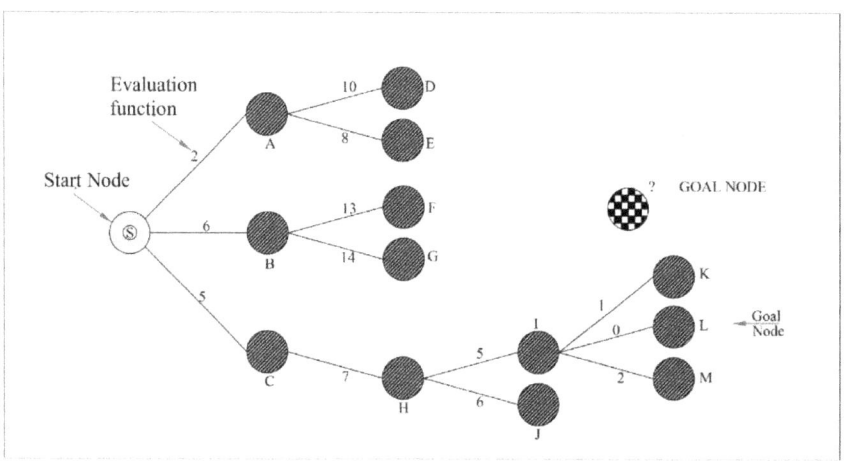

Figure 4.6 Greedy Best first search graph

How Greedy Best-First Search Works?

GBFS evaluates nodes using a heuristic function h(n)h(n)h(n), which estimates the cost to reach the goal from the current node nnn. It selects the node with the lowest h(n)h(n)h(n) value for expansion, operating under the assumption that this node is closest to the goal.

Algorithm Steps

1. **Initialization:**

    - Place the initial node in a priority queue.

    - Priority is based on the heuristic value h(n)h(n)h(n).

2. **Exploration:**

    - Remove the node with the smallest h(n)h(n)h(n) from the queue.

    - If it is the goal state, terminate and return the solution.

- If not, expand the node and add its neighbors to the queue, evaluating their heuristic values.

3. **Iteration:**

4. **Repeat the process until the queue is empty or the goal is reached.**

Heuristic Function

The heuristic function $h(n)h(n)h(n)$ is central to GBFS and must be carefully designed for the algorithm to perform efficiently. Examples of heuristic functions include:

- **Straight-Line Distance**: Used in problems like route planning, where $h(n)$ is the Euclidean distance to the goal.
- **Number of Misplaced Tiles**: In puzzles like the 8 Puzzle, $h(n)$ can count tiles out of place compared to the goal state.

Example: Navigating a Graph with GBFS`

Consider a graph representing cities, where the goal is to find the shortest route to a target city. GBFS evaluates cities based on their straight-line distance to the target and chooses the one closest to the goal for exploration.

Advantages of GBFS:

1. **Efficiency:**

   - GBFS is faster than uninformed search algorithms like Breadth-First Search (BFS) because it uses a heuristic to focus on promising paths.

2. **Focus on Goal:**

   - It prioritizes exploration toward the goal, reducing the number of nodes visited in many cases.

3. **Simple to Implement:**

   - The use of a priority queue makes GBFS relatively straightforward to code.

Disadvantages of GBFS

1. **Non-Optimal:**
   - GBFS does not guarantee finding the shortest or least-cost solution. It may choose suboptimal paths due to reliance solely on $h(n)h(n)h(n)$.

2. **Incomplete:**
   - If the heuristic leads to a dead-end or an infinite loop, GBFS may fail to find a solution unless additional mechanisms (e.g., cycle detection) are used.

3. **Heuristic Dependence:**
   - The performance of GBFS is highly dependent on the quality of the heuristic function. Poor heuristics can make the algorithm inefficient or incorrect.

Applications of GBFS

1. **Pathfinding:**
   - Used in navigation systems where speed is more critical than optimality.

Table 4.4 Comparison of GBFS with Other Algorithms

Aspect	Greedy Best-First Search	*A Search Algorithm**
Evaluation Function	$h(n)h(n)h(n)$ (heuristic estimate to goal)	$f(n)=g(n)+h(n) f(n) = g(n) + h(n) f(n)=g(n)+h(n)$ (cost so far + heuristic estimate)
Optimality	Not guaranteed	Guaranteed if $h(n)h(n)h(n)$ is admissible
Completeness	Not guaranteed	Guaranteed if a solution exists

| Focus | Focuses entirely on heuristic | Balances heuristic with path cost |

2. **Game Playing:**

    - Applied in decision-making for games like chess or puzzles to prioritize promising moves.

3. **Robotics:**

    - GBFS helps robots plan paths to target locations efficiently.

GBFS is a valuable algorithm in Artificial Intelligence (AI), offering a fast, heuristic-driven approach to problem-solving. However, its lack of optimality and completeness nice.

A* Search Algorithm

The A* search algorithm combines the benefits of Breadth-First Search (BFS) with Depth-First Search (DFS), rendering it a well-known and informed search strategy. It employs a heuristic method to efficiently explore the state space while ensuring the shortest path to the goal, assuming the heuristic is admissible (does not overestimate the cost).

How A* Search Works?

A* uses an evaluation function f(n)f(n)f(n) to determine the priority of nodes for exploration. The evaluation function is defined as:

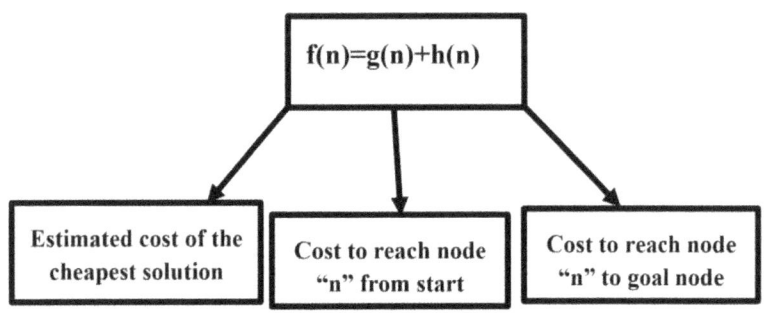

Figure 4.7 Evaluation function f(n) in A* Algorithm

Where:

- $g(n)$: The cost of the path from the start node to the current node nnn.

- $h(n)$: A heuristic estimate of the cost from nnn to the goal node.

The algorithm selects nodes with the lowest (n), ensuring a balance between the actual and anticipated costs to reach the goal.

A* Algorithm Steps

1. **Initialization:**
   - Create a priority queue (open list) and add the start node with its $f(n)$ value.
   - Maintain a closed list to track explored nodes.

2. **Node Expansion:**
   - Dequeue the node with the lowest $f(n)$ from the open list.
   - If the node is the goal, terminate and reconstruct the path.

3. **Successor Generation:**
   - Generate all successors of the current node.
   - Calculate $g(n)$, $h(n)$, and $f(n)$ for each successor.

4. **Update Open List:**
   - If a successor is not in the open or closed list, add it to the open list.
   - If a successor is already in the open list with a higher $f(n)$, update it with the lower value.

5. **Repeat:**
   - Continue until the goal is reached or the open list is empty (indicating no solution exists).

Key Properties of A*

1. **Admissibility:**
   - A* is admissible if the heuristic $h(n)$ is non-overestimating, ensuring it finds an optimal solution.

2. **Consistency (Monotonicity):**
   - A consistent heuristic satisfies $h(n) \leq c(n,n') + h(n')$, where $c(n,n')$ is the cost of transitioning between nodes n and n'. Consistency guarantees that $f(n)$ values are non-decreasing along a path.

3. **Optimality:**
   - A* guarantees an optimal solution if the heuristic is admissible and consistent.

Advantages of A*

1. **Efficiency:**
   - A* intelligently explores the most promising paths first, reducing unnecessary exploration.

2. **Guaranteed Optimality:**
   - Finds the shortest path to the goal if the heuristic is admissible.

3. **Flexible Heuristics:**
   - Heuristics can be tailored to specific problems for improved performance.

Disadvantages of A*

1. **Memory Intensive:**
   - A* stores all explored and frontier nodes, which can lead to high memory usage for large problems.

2. Heuristic Sensitivity:

- The efficiency of A* heavily depends on the quality of the heuristic function. Poor heuristics can result in suboptimal performance.

Applications of A*

1. Pathfinding:

- Widely used in games and robotics for finding optimal paths.
- Example: Navigating through a maze or map.

2. Puzzle Solving:

- Used for solving problems like the 8 Puzzle and 15 Puzzle.

3. Route Planning:

- Applied in GPS systems for determining the shortest or fastest route between locations.

Example: Solving the 8 Puzzle 8 Puzzle problem, with A*

A* uses a heuristic such as the **Manhattan distance** or misplaced tiles to estimate the number of moves required to reach the goal state.

- Start State: Initial configuration of the puzzle.
- Goal State: Target configuration (e.g., tiles arranged in order).
- Heuristic (h(n)): The sum of the distances of each tile from its target position (Manhattan distance).

By evaluating $f(n)=g(n)+h(n)$ for each state, A* systematically explores configurations, prioritizing those with the lowest estimated total cost.

Table 4.5 Comparison of A* with Other Algorithms

Aspect	A*	BFS	DFS
Completeness	Guaranteed	Guaranteed	Not guaranteed in infinite spaces
Optimality	Guaranteed with admissible heuristic	Guaranteed for uniform-cost problems	Not guaranteed
Memory Efficiency	High memory usage	High memory usage	Low memory usage
Heuristic Use	Utilizes heuristics	Does not use heuristics	Does not use heuristics

A* is one of the most versatile and effective search algorithms, balancing exploration and exploitation using heuristics. Its applications in AI, robotics, and game development make it a cornerstone of intelligent systems.

Key Terms in A* Search

- g(n)g(n)g(n): The cost to reach the current state nnn.
- h(n)h(n)h(n): A heuristic estimate of the cost to reach the goal from nnn.
- f(n)=g(n)+h(n). The total cost function combining actual cost and heuristic estimate.

Examples and Applications of Search Strategies and Problem-solving agents

To understand search strategies, we examine several classical problems:

What is 8 Puzzle Problem in AI and Its Relevance?

8 Puzzle Problem in AI

The 8-puzzle, often regarded as a small, solvable piece of a larger puzzle, holds a central place in AI because of its relevance in understanding and developing algorithms for more complex problems. In 8 puzzle, the empty block can be in the middle, or corner or along an edge. When the empty tile is in the middle, four moves are possible; when it is in a corner, two; and when it is along an edge, three

Rules and Constraints:
To tackle the 8-puzzle, it's crucial to comprehend its rules and constraints:

- The 8-puzzle is typically played on a 3x3 grid, which provides a 3x3 square arrangement for tiles. This grid structure is fundamental to the problem's organization.

- The puzzle comprises 8 numbered tiles (usually from 1 to 8) and one blank tile. These numbered tiles can be slid into adjacent positions (horizontally or vertically) when there's an available space, which is occupied by the blank tile, namely

- Move the blank space up.

- Move the blank space down.

- Move the blank space left.

- Move the blank space right.

- The objective of the 8-puzzle is to transform an initial state, defined by the arrangement of the tiles on the grid, into a specified goal state. The goal state is often a predefined configuration, such as having the tiles arranged in ascending order from left to right and top to bottom, with the blank tile in the bottom-right corner.

The 8-puzzle consists of eight numbered tiles arranged in a 3×3 grid with one empty cell. The goal is to reach a specific configuration by sliding tiles into the empty space. This problem demonstrates:

- State space: All possible arrangements of tiles

- Actions: Moving tiles adjacent to the empty space

- Goal test: Checking if current configuration matches target

The solution to the problem requires rearranging the tiles from the initial state to the goal state by making a series of these legal moves.

Problem Representation

In AI, the 8 Puzzle Problem is typically represented as a state space problem:

- State: A specific configuration of the tiles on the grid. Each unique arrangement of tiles is considered a distinct state.
- Action: A legal move that changes the position of the blank space and an adjacent tile.
- Goal Test: A condition that checks whether the current state matches the goal configuration.
- Cost: Each move has a uniform cost, typically 1 per move, making this an instance of a uniform cost search problem.

A. Solving the 8 Puzzle Problem

The 8 Puzzle problem involves finding a sequence of moves to transition from the initial state to the goal state. Various AI search algorithms are used to explore the state space, such as breadth-first search (BFS), depth-first search (DFS), and the A* search algorithm. Table 4.5 provides a detailed comparison of these algorithms with their advantages and disadvantages.

8 Puzzle Initial and Final States

Initial State

2	8	3
1		4
7	6	5

Final State

1	2	3
8		4
7	6	5

8 Puzzle Initial State and Possible moves

2	8	3
1		4
7	6	5

Move 6 Up
Move 8 down
Move 4 Left
Move 1 right

Initial State

7	2	4
5		6
8	3	1

Final State

	1	2
3	4	5
6	7	8

Figure 4.8 8-Puzzle: Initial State and Possible Moves

Table 4.6: Comparison of Search Algorithms for Solving the 8 Puzzle Problem

Search Algorithm	Description	Advantages	Disadvantages
Breadth-First Search (BFS)	An uninformed search algorithm that explores all states level by level, starting from the initial state. Ensures the shortest path is found in terms of moves.	- Guarantees the optimal solution (shortest number of moves).	- High memory requirement as all states at each level must be stored.
Depth-First Search (DFS)	Another uninformed search algorithm that explores one branch deeply before backtracking to explore others. Does	- More memory-efficient than BFS.	- May get stuck in deep, non-optimal paths and may not

			not guarantee the shortest solution.		find the shortest solution.
A* Search Algorithm	A heuristic search algorithm that uses a priority queue to explore the most promising states first, guided by the evaluation function f(n)=g(n)+h(n)f(n) = g(n) + h(n)f(n)=g(n)+h(n).	- Combines the efficiency of DFS and BFS. newline - Guarantees the shortest path if an admissible heuristic is used.	- Can be slow if the heuristic is not well-designed.

This comparison highlights how different algorithms approach the problem and their trade-offs in solving the 8 Puzzle.

The average solution cost for a randomly generated 8-puzzle instance is approximately 22 steps. The branching factor is around 3, as the empty tile can have four possible moves when in the center, three when along an edge, and two when in a corner. Consequently, an exhaustive tree search to depth 22 would evaluate about $3^{22} \approx 3.1 \times 10$.

Using a graph search significantly reduces this number by eliminating duplicate states. For the 8-puzzle, only $9!/2 = 181,440$ distinct states are reachable due to constraints, reducing the number of states by a factor of approximately 170,000. While this is a manageable size, the corresponding number for the 15-puzzle is around 10^{13}, necessitating an efficient heuristic function to solve the problem optimally.

To find the shortest solutions using the A* algorithm, we require a heuristic function that never overestimates the number of steps to the goal, ensuring admissibility. Two commonly used heuristics for the 15-puzzle are:

1. **Misplaced Tiles Heuristic (h_1):**

    h_1, *represents a heuristic*, such as the number of misplaced tiles counts the number of tiles that are not in their correct positions. For example, in a given initial state, if all eight tiles are misplaced, h1=8. This heuristic is admissible because any tile out of place must be moved at least once to reach its goal position.

2. **Manhattan Distance Heuristic (h_2):**

    h_2, *rrepresents* a heuristic, such as the Manhattan distance. calculates the sum of the distances of tiles from their goal positions, using the horizontal and vertical distances only (diagonal moves are not allowed). This is also referred to as the city block distance. For instance, in a start state, if the sum of the distances for all tiles is:

    $$h_2=3+1+2+2+2+3+3+2=18$$

This heuristic is admissible because each move reduces the Manhattan distance by at most one step.

Both h_1 and h_2 guide the A* search algorithm effectively, with h_2 generally providing better performance due to its more accurate estimation of the remaining cost to the goal.

Chapter Summary and Concluding Thoughts

In this chapter elaborated the concepts on uninformed and informed search strategies. Uninformed search strategies such as Breadth-First Search (BFS), Depth-First Search (DFS), Iterative Deepening Depth-First Search (IDDFS), and Bidirectional Depth-First Search. Informed search strategies such as Greedy Best-First Search (GBFS) and the versatile A* search algorithm.

Each strategy was explored with advantages, limitations, applications, and comparisons, highlighting their distinct strengths and weaknesses in handling various sorts of problems.

Real-world applications, such as solving the 8-puzzle, demonstrated the actual implementation of different search strategies, highlighting the significance of choosing the appropriate algorithm based on the nature and restrictions of the problem. grasp the trade-offs between these approaches helps readers obtain a better grasp of how Artificial Intelligence systems solve complicated issues efficiently.

These topics provide a solid basis for future chapters, which will delve into more complex AI techniques and applications, bridging the gap between fundamental notions and real-world problem resolution.

Artificial Intelligence for Undergraduate Students

Chapter – 5
Knowledge Based Agents and Logical Reasoning

Knowledge–based agents, The Wumpus world, Logic, Propositional logic, Reasoning patterns in Propositional Logic. Syntax and Semantics of First Order logic, Using First Order logic. Inference in First Order Logic: Propositional Versus First Order Inference, Unification, Forward Chaining, Backward Chaining, Resolution.

1. **Knowledge-Based Agents**: How agents use stored knowledge to make decisions.
2. **The Wumpus World**: A classic example to illustrate reasoning under uncertainty.
3. **Logic and Propositional Logic**: Basics of logical systems and reasoning patterns.
4. **First-Order Logic (FOL)**: Syntax, semantics, and applications of FOL in AI.
5. **Inference in Logic**: Techniques like unification, forward chaining, backward chaining, and resolution, comparing propositional and first-order inference methods.

Knowledge-Based Agents:

Knowledge-based agents are a type of intelligent agent that leverages stored knowledge to make informed decisions and solve problems. These agents rely on a **knowledge base (KB)**, which is a structured repository of facts, rules, and information about their environment. The knowledge base is used in conjunction with an inference engine to derive new information and make decisions. Intelligent agents require knowledge about the real world to make decisions and reason efficiently. **Knowledge-based agents** are a specialized type of intelligent agents with the ability to:

- Maintain an internal state of knowledge.
- Reason over that knowledge to draw conclusions.
- Update their knowledge base based on observations.
- Take informed actions accordingly.

These agents use a **formal representation** of the world to reason and act intelligently. They are composed of two primary components:

1. **Knowledge Base (KB):**

- A structured repository of facts, rules, and information about the world.
- Enables the agent to store and retrieve knowledge for reasoning.

2. **Inference System:**

- A mechanism to apply logical reasoning to the knowledge base.
- Allows the agent to deduce new facts, resolve uncertainties, and identify appropriate actions.

Capabilities of a Knowledge-Based Agent

A knowledge-based agent must possess the following capabilities:

- Representation: It should represent states, actions, and other world elements using a formal language.

- Incorporation of New Precepts: It should update its knowledge base dynamically with new information from the environment.

- Internal Representation Updates: It should refine its internal model of the world as new observations are made.

- Reasoning: It should deduce facts and infer the state of the world based on available knowledge.

- Action Deduction: It should determine and execute appropriate actions based on its reasoning process.

This combination of knowledge representation, reasoning, and decision-making allows knowledge-based agents to act intelligently and adapt to complex environments.

Key features of knowledge-based agents include:

1. **Knowledge Representation:**

- The agent uses formal languages (e.g., propositional or first-order logic) to represent facts and rules.

- This allows for reasoning about the environment in a structured and interpretable way.

2. **Decision-Making:**

- Based on the stored knowledge, the agent evaluates possible actions and selects the one that aligns with its goals.

- The reasoning process involves applying inference techniques to deduce new facts or resolve uncertainties.

3. **Dynamic Updates:**

- The agent continuously updates its knowledge base as it perceives new information from the environment.

- This makes the agent adaptable and capable of handling dynamic scenarios.

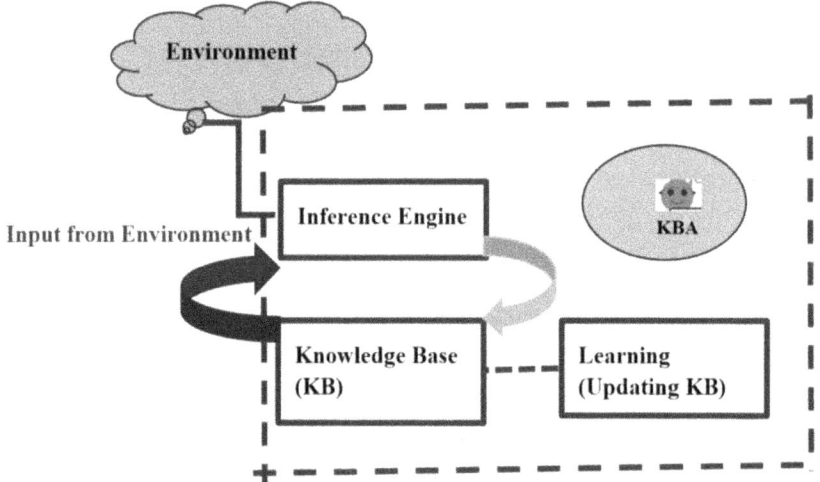

Figure 5.1 The Knowledge-Based Agent Architecture

Operations Performed by KBA

Following are three operations which are performed by KBA in order to show the intelligent behaviour:

1. **TELL:** This operation tells the knowledge base what it perceives from the environment.

2. **ASK:** This operation asks the knowledge base what action it should perform.

3. **Perform:** It performs the selected action.

Knowledge Base (KB):

The **knowledge base** is a central component of a knowledge-based agent (KBA)} and is often referred to as KB. It is a collection of **sentences** *(a technical term distinct from sentences in natural language)* that represent facts about the world. These sentences are expressed in a structured **knowledge representation language** Knowledge Representation Language, enabling the agent to store and manipulate knowledge systematically.

Why Use a Knowledge Base?

A knowledge base is essential for:

- Updating Knowledge: It allows the agent to incorporate new information from its environment.

- Learning from Experience: The KB evolves as the agent interacts with the world.

- Informed Decision-Making: Actions are guided by the accumulated and processed knowledge in the KB.

Inference System

The **inference system** is responsible for deriving new sentences from existing ones in the knowledge base (KB). This process, known as **inference**, enables the agent to expand its understanding and take appropriate actions. A sentence, in this context, is a proposition or assertion about the world.

The inference system applies **logical rules** to the KB, deducing new information that the agent can use to update its knowledge base and reason about the world effectively.

Working of the Inference System

The inference system operates using two primary methods:

1. **Forward Chaining**

   - Starts with known facts in the KB and applies inference rules to deduce new facts.

   - Useful for deriving all possible conclusions from given knowledge.

2. **Backward Chaining**

   - Begins with a goal or query and works backward to determine if the goal can be satisfied using the knowledge in the KB.

- Efficient for answering specific questions or achieving targeted objectives.

By integrating the **knowledge base** and **inference system**, a knowledge-based agent can effectively reason, learn, and act in dynamic environments, ensuring intelligent behaviour.

Examples of Knowledge-Based Agents (KBA)

1. **Medical Diagnosis System**

    - Use Case: A system used by healthcare professionals to diagnose diseases.

    - Knowledge Base: Contains medical facts, symptoms, diseases, and their relationships (e.g., "Fever and rash suggest measles").

    - Inference System: Uses forward chaining to analyze symptoms and deduce potential diseases, or backward chaining to verify a suspected diagnosis.

    - Example in Action: A patient reports fever and fatigue. The system infers possible conditions like flu or dengue, and suggests tests for confirmation.

2. **Virtual Personal Assistants**

3. **Use Case: Virtual assistants like Siri, Alexa, or Google Assistant.**

4. **Knowledge Base: Stores information about user preferences, tasks, weather, and events.**

    - Inference System: Infers appropriate actions, such as setting a reminder when you say, "Remind me to call John tomorrow at 10 AM."

    - **Example in Action: If the user asks, "Do I have any meetings today?" the system checks the knowledge base (calendar entries) and responds accordingly.**

5. **The Wumpus World Game**

    - Use Case: A classic AI environment for reasoning under uncertainty.

    - Knowledge Base: Facts about the environment (e.g., "Breeze indicates a pit nearby").

    - Inference System: Uses forward chaining to deduce the safest path and backward chaining to determine if a specific location is safe.

    - Example in Action: The agent perceives a breeze in a square, infers that a pit is in one of the adjacent squares, and avoids stepping into those areas.

6. **Fraud Detection Systems**

    - Use Case: Banking systems to identify fraudulent transactions.

    - Knowledge Base: Rules about legitimate and suspicious activities (e.g., "High-value transactions from unusual locations may indicate fraud").

    - Inference System: Applies these rules to deduce whether a transaction is legitimate or fraudulent.

    - Example in Action: A credit card is used in two different countries within minutes. The system flags the transaction as suspicious and notifies the user.

7. **Automated Customer Support**

    - Use Case: Chatbots for answering user queries.

    - Knowledge Base: Stores frequently asked questions, solutions, and procedures.

    - Inference System: Matches user queries to the most relevant answers and infers follow-up questions for clarification.

- Example in Action: A user asks, "How do I reset my password?" The chatbot retrieves the relevant steps from the KB and provides guidance.

These examples demonstrate how knowledge-based agents utilize their knowledge base and inference system to reason and act intelligently in various domains.

The Wumpus World

The **Wumpus World** is a classic problem in artificial intelligence used to illustrate reasoning under uncertainty, the design of knowledge-based agents, and the use of logical inference. It is a grid-based environment where an agent navigates a world filled with hazards, aiming to achieve its goal while avoiding dangers.

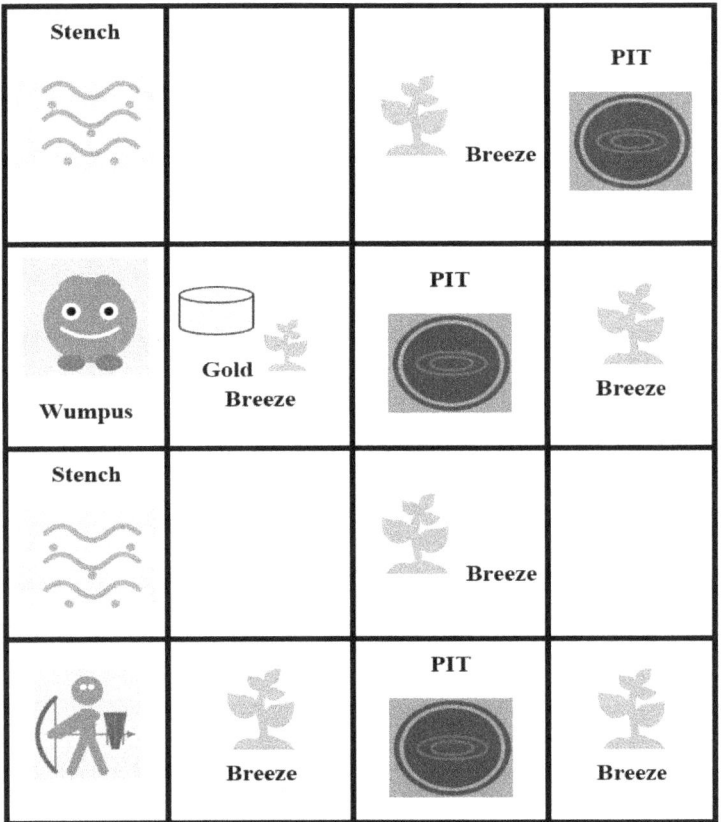

Figure 5.2 The Wumpus World (4x4 grid)

Components of the Wumpus World

1. **Grid Environment:**

   - The world is a square grid (e.g., 4x4), and each cell can contain objects or hazards.

2. **Objects and Hazards:**

   - **Agent:** The player-controlled entity that explores the grid.
   - **Gold:** The goal of the game; the agent must locate and retrieve the gold.
   - **Pits:** Deadly holes falling into a pit results in the agent's death.
   - **Wumpus:** A dangerous monster that kills the agent if entered into its cell.

3. **Precepts:**

   - **Breeze:** Felt in a cell adjacent to a pit.
   - **Bump:** Experienced when the agent tries to move into a wall.
   - **Glitter:** Observed in a cell containing gold
   - **Scream:** Heard when the Wumpus is killed by the agent.
   - **Stench:** Detected in a cell adjacent to the Wumpus.

Goal of the Agent

The agent's objective is to locate and retrieve the gold while avoiding pits and the Wumpus. After finding the gold, the agent must return safely to its starting position.

1. **Agent Actions:**

   - Move forward
   - Turn left or right

- Grab the gold
- Shoot an arrow (to potentially kill the Wumpus)

2. **Strategy Considerations:**

   - The agent must use logical reasoning and probabilistic inference
   - Must map the world with limited sensory information
   - Needs to avoid deadly squares
   - Balance exploration with safety

PEAS Description of the Wumpus World

The **Wumpus World** can be described using the **PEAS framework**, which defines the Performance measure, Environment, Actuators, and Sensors of an agent. This framework helps outline the agent's objectives and its interactions with the environment.

Performance Measure

The agent's success in the Wumpus World is evaluated using the following performance measures:

- **+1000 points**: Reward for safely exiting the cave with the gold.
- **-1000 points**: Penalty for being eaten by the Wumpus or falling into a pit.
- **-1 point**: Penalty for each action taken (e.g., moving, turning).
- **-10 points**: Penalty for using an arrow to attempt killing the Wumpus.

The game ends when either:

- The agent successfully escapes with the gold.
- The agent dies by encountering the Wumpus or falling into a pit.

This performance measure incentivizes efficient, cautious exploration and prioritizes the agent's survival and task completion.

3. **Implementation Techniques**

   - Often solved using:
   - Propositional logic
   - First-order logic
   - Probabilistic reasoning algorithms
   - Search algorithms like A*

Reasoning in the Wumpus World

The Wumpus World requires the agent to use logical reasoning to deduce the safest and most efficient path. The agent must update its **knowledge base** based on its **precepts** and make decisions using the **inference system**

4. **Forward Chaining:**

   Starts with known facts (e.g., "Breeze is felt in this cell") and infers the possible locations of pits.

5. **Backward Chaining:**

   Starts with a goal (e.g., "Is it safe to move to cell [2,2]?") and works backward using rules to verify safety.

Example Scenario

1. The agent starts in a corner of the grid.
2. It perceives a **breeze**, indicating one or more pits in adjacent cells.
3. Using logical inference, the agent deduces the possible locations of pits and marks them as dangerous.
4. It perceives a **stench** near another cell, inferring the Wumpus's possible location.
5. It avoids dangerous cells, locates the **gold**, and safely returns to the starting point.

The **Wumpus World** is a powerful tool for teaching knowledge-based reasoning, decision-making, and the integration of perceptual data into an agent's behaviour. It demonstrates how agents use a combination of their **knowledge base**, **precepts**, and **logical inference** to act intelligently in uncertain environments.

Logic and Propositional Logic in the Context of AI and AI Agents

Logic is the study of reasoning and formal systems of thought. In artificial intelligence (AI), logic provides a foundational framework for representing knowledge, reasoning, and enabling intelligent agents to make decisions. Logic allows agents to process facts, deduce new information, and take actions in a structured and interpretable way.

Logic in AI:

Logic in AI focuses on creating systems that can emulate human reasoning. It is used to formalize how AI agents represent knowledge about their environment and reason about it. Logic ensures that an AI agent's decisions are consistent, rational, and explainable.

Types of Logic in AI:

1. **Propositional Logic:**

    - Deals with propositions (statements) and their relationships using logical connectives.

    - Example: "If the sky is clear, then it is not raining."

2. **First-Order Logic (FOL):**

    - Extends propositional logic by including quantifiers and relations between objects.

    - Example: "For all people, if someone is a student, they attend classes."

3. **Modal Logic:**

4. **Represents possibilities, necessities, or beliefs.**

- Example: "It is possible that the agent will win the game."

5. **Temporal Logic:**

    - Focuses on reasoning about time-based events.
    - Example: "If the alarm rings, the agent will leave the building within 5 minutes."

6. **Fuzzy Logic:**

    - Handles reasoning under uncertainty with degrees of truth rather than binary true/false values.
    - Example: "The weather is somewhat sunny today.", "The weather is moderately warm."

Reasoning in AI: Deductive, Inductive, and Abductive Logics

AI agents employ different types of reasoning, depending on the problem context and the nature of available information.

1. **Deductive Reasoning:**

    - Derives logically certain conclusions from general rules and specific facts.
    - Example in AI:
      ❖ Rule: "All humans are mortal."
      ❖ Fact: "Socrates is a human."
      ❖ Conclusion: "Socrates is mortal."
        - Deductive reasoning is common in knowledge-based systems where certainty is required.

2. **Inductive Reasoning:**

    - Generalizes patterns or rules from specific observations.
    - Example in AI:

- ❖ Observations: "The sun rose today, yesterday, and the day before."
- ❖ Conclusion: "The sun rises every day."
  - Inductive reasoning is used in machine learning to identify patterns in data.

3. **Abductive Reasoning:**
   - Infers the most plausible explanation for an observation.
   - Example in AI:
   - ❖ Observation: "The ground is wet."
   - ❖ Hypothesis: "It rained."
   - ❖ Abductive reasoning is common in diagnostic systems and hypothesis generation.

Propositional logic, Reasoning patterns in Propositional Logic:
Propositional Logic is a formal system used for reasoning about propositions (statements) and their relationships. In artificial intelligence (AI), propositional logic provides a foundation for creating rules and reasoning systems, enabling AI agents to make decisions and draw conclusions based on facts.

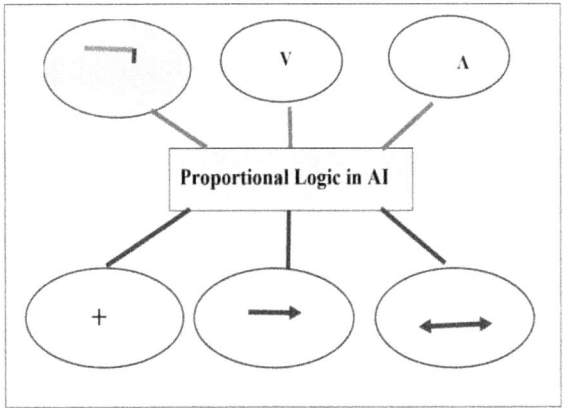

Figure 5.3 Logical Connectives of Propositional Logic

Propositions: A **proposition** is a declarative statement that can be either **true** or **false**, but not both.

Example:
- p: "The light is on."
- q: "The room is empty."

Propositional Variables
- Propositional logic uses variables (e.g., p,q,r,s) to represent propositions.
- Each variable can hold a truth value:
- **True** (T) or
- **False** (F).

Propositional Connectives
Propositional connectives are symbols used to combine or modify propositions to express logical relationships. These connectives are fundamental in programming AI agents to evaluate and act based on logical conditions.

Common Propositional Connectives:

1. **Negation (¬)**
   1. Represents "NOT."
   2. If p is true, ¬p (not p) is false, and vice versa.
   3. **Example**: If p = "It is raining," ¬p = "It is not raining."

2. **Conjunction (∧)**
   1. Represents "AND."
   2. True only when both propositions are true.
   3. Example: p∧q = "The light is on AND the room is empty."

3. **Disjunction (∨)**
    1. Represents "OR."
    2. True if at least one of the propositions is true.
    3. Example: p∨q = "The light is on OR the room is empty."

4. **Implication (→)**
    1. Represents "IF...THEN."
    2. p→q: If p is true, then q must be true. If p is false, the implication is always true.
    3. Example: "If it is raining (p), then the ground is wet (q)."

5. **Biconditional (↔) Biconditional (↔}**
    1. Represents "IF AND ONLY IF."
    2. True when both propositions are either true or false.
    3. Example: p↔q = "The light is on IF AND ONLY IF the room is empty."

Propositional Logic in AI Agents

Propositional logic is used in AI agents to encode rules and reason about the world.

How It Works?

1. **Representation of Rules:**
    1. Rules are encoded using propositional logic.
    2. Example: "If there is a stench (p), then there is a Wumpus nearby (q)" is written as p→q .

2. **Inference:**

    1. AI agents use inference systems (e.g., forward chaining or backward chaining) to derive conclusions from a knowledge base.

    2. Example: If p (stench is detected), infer q (Wumpus is nearby).

3. **Decision-Making:**

    1. Logical connectives help agents evaluate multiple conditions.

    2. **Example: "Move to a cell only if it is safe ($\neg p \wedge \neg q$)"**

Summary of Key Points

- **Propositions:** Statements that are either true or false.
- **Connectives:** Combine propositions to represent complex rules and conditions.
    - $\neg$: Negation (NOT).
    - $\wedge$: Conjunction (AND).
    - $\vee$: Disjunction (OR).
    - $\rightarrow$: Implication (IF...THEN).
    - $\leftrightarrow$: Biconditional (IF AND ONLY IF).

Usage in AI:

- Represent knowledge about the environment.
- Enable logical inference for decision-making.
- Program rules for AI agents to reason effectively.

This logical framework enables AI systems to analyze, reason, and act based on a structured representation of the world.

First Order logic (FOL) in AI

First-Order Logic (FOL), also known as **First-Order Predicate Logic**, is a fundamental theoretical framework that has widespread use in fields such as mathematics, philosophy, computer science, and linguistics. It provides a useful framework for expressing and reasoning about the relationships between items in a given domain. FOL broadens/expands propositional logic by including objects, connections, and quantifiers. FOL is more expressive than propositional logic, enabling for the structured representation of complicated/complex facts and reasoning. It is frequently employed in AI for knowledge representation, reasoning, and intelligent system design.

In the discipline of artificial intelligence (AI), **First-Order Logic (FOL)**, is a foundation/ corner stone for knowledge representation and reasoning. FOL's well-defined syntax and semantics enable the precise storing of information and relationships, making it a reliable/trustworthy tool for AI systems. For example, FOL is utilized in automated reasoning planning and natural language understanding, where its expressiveness permits complex problem-solving and decision-making.

Key Components of FOL

1. **Objects**:

    - Entities in the domain of discourse (e.g., people, places, things).
    - Example: "Socrates," "Athens," "Gold.", "Rama", "Bangalore", "Mercury"

Element	Example
Constants	Numbers (1, 2, 3), Named objects (john, paris), Special values (π, e) Lakshmi, Jagannadh, cow
Variables	x, y, z, n - used as placeholders for values that can vary
Predicates	Parent(x,y) - "x is parent of y"
Functions	sqrt(x), average(x,y), sum(x,y), max(x,y)
Symbols	? (AND), ? (OR), ? (IMPLIES), ¬ (NOT), ? (IF AND ONLY IF)
Equality	= (equals), ? (not equals), = (less than or equal), = (greater than or equal)
Quantifiers	? (For all), ? (There exists)

Figure 5.4 Basic First-Order Logic Elements

2. **Predicates** FOL:

Represent relationships or properties of objects.

Example:

- ❖ Human(Socrates): "Socrates is a human."
- ❖ LivesIn(Socrates, Athens): "Socrates lives in Athens."
- ❖ LivesIn(Rama, Bangalore): "Rama lives in Bangalore"

3. Constants:

- Specific objects in the domain.
- Example: "Socrates," "Athens."

4. Variables:

- Represent arbitrary elements in the domain.

- Example: x,y,z.

5. **Quantifiers** in FOL:

Enable reasoning about groups or subsets of objects:

- **Universal Quantifier (∀\forall∀): "For all."**
  - ❖ ∀x Human(x): "All x are humans."
- **Existential Quantifier (∃): "There exists."**
  - ❖ ∃ x LivesIn(x,Athens): "There exists an xxx who lives in Athens."
  - ❖ ∃x StudiesIn(x,Don Bosco Institute of Technology)

1. **Logical Connectives**:

Same as in propositional logic: ¬, ∧, ∨, →, ↔

2. **DFS Functions**:

Map objects to other objects.

Example: ParentOf(x): "Parent of x."

GrandParentOf(g,x)

Interpretation: "g" is the grandparent of x."

Here, g is the grandparent, and x is the grandchild.

This representation explicitly connects the grandparent and the grandchild.

Example: Using Parent Relationships:

If the grandparent relationship is derived from the parent relationship:

∃p (ParentOf(g,p)∧ParentOf(p,x))

- **Interpretation:**
  "There exists p such that g is the parent of p, and p is the parent of x."

- This representation explicitly defines a grandparent relationship in terms of intermediate parent relationships.

In table 5.1 summary for FOL logic components is presented.

Table 5.1 Summary for First-Order Logic Components

Component	Symbol	Name	Description	Example
Universal Quantifier	$\forall$	For All	Asserts that a predicate is true for all elements in the domain	$\forall x\ (P(x))$
Existential Quantifier	$\exists$	There Exists	Asserts that there is at least one element in the domain for which the predicate is true	$\exists x\ (P(x))$
Predicate	$P(x)$	Predicate	A function that returns true or false based on the object(s) it is applied to	$P(x)$: "x is a person"
Conjunction	$\wedge$	AND	True if both predicates are true	$P(x) \wedge Q(x)$
Disjunction	$\vee$	OR	True if at least one of the predicates is true	$P(x) \vee Q(x)$
Negation	$\neg$	NOT	True if the predicate is false	$\neg P(x)$
Implication	$\rightarrow$	IMPLIES	True if the first predicate implies the	$P(x) \rightarrow Q(x)$

			second predicate	
Biconditional	↔	BICONDITIONAL	True if both predicates are either true or false	P(x) ↔ Q(x)

Syntax of First-Order Logic

The **syntax** defines the rules for constructing valid expressions in FOL. It specifies how symbols (constants, variables, predicates, connectives, quantifiers) can be combined.

Atomic Sentences

- **Predicates applied to terms:**
  ❖ Example: Loves(Socrates, Philosophy): "Socrates loves philosophy."
  ❖ Loves(Jagannadh, Artificial Intelligent Agents): Jagannadh loves Artificial Intelligent Agents

Breakdown of the Predicate

1. **Predicate Name:**

   - **Loves: Represents the relationship of "loving."**

2. **Arguments:**

   - Jagannadh: The subject (an individual or constant in the domain).

   - Artificial Intelligent Agents: The object being loved (a constant or entity in the domain).

3. **Interpretation:**

   - The predicate asserts that the relationship LovesLovesLoves holds between Jagannadh and ArtificiaIntelligent Agents.

- It can be read as "Jagannadh loves Artificial Intelligent Agents."

Complex Sentences

4. **Formed using logical connectives and quantifiers:**
   - Example: $\forall x\ (Human(x) \rightarrow Mortal(x))$:

     "All humans are mortal."

Well-Formed Formulas (WFFs) in First-Order Logic

Well-formed formulas (WFFs) in First-Order Logic (FOL) are expressions which meet/satisfy the syntactic rules of FOL. They express meaningful assertions about the world and constitute the basic building blocks for encoding knowledge and reasoning in artificial intelligence (AI) systems. Well-formed formulas (WFFs) in First-Order Logic (FOL) are expressions that follow the syntactic rules of FOL. They express meaningful assertions about the world and are the basic building blocks for encoding knowledge and reasoning in artificial intelligence (AI) systems.

Characteristics of WFFs

5. **Syntax Compliance:**
   - WFFs adhere strictly to the syntactic rules of FOL, defining how terms, predicates, quantifiers, and logical connectives can combine to form valid expressions.

Symbolic Representation:

6. **WFFs consist of:**
   - **Terms**: Constants, variables, and functions.
   - **Predicates**: Represent relationships or properties of terms.
   - **Quantifiers**: Universal ($\forall$\forall$\forall$) and existential ($\exists$\exists$\exists$).
   - Logical Connectives: Logical connectives include conjunction AND ($\wedge$), disjunction OR ($\vee$), implication IMPLIES ($\rightarrow$), and negation NOT ($\neg$), which are used to combine or modify logical statements.

1. **Quantifier Scope**

- WFFs clearly define the scope of quantifiers, ensuring variables are appropriately bound within the formula.
- Example:
- ∀x(Human(x)→Mortal(x)): "For all xxx, if xxx is a human, then xxx is mortal."

2. **Complexity and Nesting**:

- WFFs can range from simple atomic formulas to complex nested expressions involving multiple quantifiers and connectives.
- Proper nesting ensures unambiguous interpretation.
- Example:
  ❖ ∀x∃y(Loves(x,y)∧Friend(y,x)): "For every x, there exists a y such that x loves y, and y is a friend of x."

Importance of Well-Formed Formulas

1. **Knowledge Representation:**

- WFFs provide a formal language to represent knowledge about the world.
- They enable the encoding of facts, rules, constraints, and relationships in a structured and precise manner.

Example:

❖ Parent(Suryanarayana, Rajalakshmi) ∧ Female(Rajalakshmi)

  " Suryanarayana is Rajalakshmi's parent, and Rajalakshmi is female."

2. **Automated Reasoning:**

- AI systems use WFFs for reasoning tasks like deduction, inference, and decision-making.

- WFFs enable the application of formal logic to derive new knowledge from existing information.

Example:

❖ From ∀x (Human(x) → Mortal(x)) and Human(Suryanarayana), infer Mortal(Suryanarayana).

3. **Semantic Understanding:**

❖ WFFs are critical for natural language processing (NLP) systems.

❖ Mapping natural language statements to logical representations involves constructing well-formed formulas.

❖ Example: Translating "Every cat is a mammal" into ∀x(Cat(x)→Mammal(x)).

4. **Problem-Solving and Planning:**

WFFs play a vital role in AI planning by defining:

❖ **Initial State**: At(Robot, Start)

❖ **Goal State**: At (Robot, Destination).

❖ **Transition Rules**: Move(x,y)→ at(Robot,y).

- Logical constraints and objectives in WFF form enable automated planning algorithms to operate effectively.

Well-formed formulas (WFFs) are syntactically valid expressions that represent knowledge in FOL. They enable AI systems to perform tasks like **knowledge representation**, **automated reasoning**, **semantic understanding**, and **planning**. Understanding the **syntax compliance**, **symbolic representation**, **quantifier scope**, and **complexity** of WFFs is critical for building robust AI systems capable of logical reasoning and problem-solving.

Semantics of First-Order Logic (FOL):
The semantics of First-Order Logic (FOL) defines the meaning of its symbols and sentences. It determines whether a sentence is true or false

in a particular interpretation in FOL, providing a formal framework for understanding and reasoning about the relationships between objects in a domain.

Key Components of Semantics in FOL

1. **Domain of Discourse:**

    - The domain is the set of all objects under consideration.
    - Every variable in FOL ranges over the domain.
    - Example:
    ❖ Domain: All humans.

2. **Interpretation:**

    - An interpretation assigns meanings to the symbols used in FOL.
    - Components of an interpretation include:
    ❖ **Constants** in FOL: Mapped to specific objects in the domain.
    ❖ Example: John → "John Smith."

    - Predicates Defined as relationships or properties over the domain.
    ❖ Example: Loves(x,y) True if x loves y.

    - **Functions Maps elements of the domain to other elements.**
    ❖ Example: Parent Of(x): Returns the parent of x.

3. **Atomic Sentences Atomic Sentences in FOL:**

    - An atomic sentence $P(t_1,t_2,...,t_n)$ is true if the relationship denoted by PPP holds for the objects denoted by $t_1,t_2,...,t_n$)
    - Example: Parent(John, Mary) is true if "John is the parent of Mary" in the given interpretation.

4. **Logical Connectives in FOL Semantics:**

   - **The truth value of complex formulas depends on their connectives:**
   - ❖ ¬ϕ: True if ϕ is false.
   - ❖ ϕ∧ψ: True if both ϕ and ψ are true.
   - ❖ ϕ∨ψ: True if at least one of ϕψ true.
   - ❖ ϕ→ψ: True if ϕ or ψ is true.
   - ❖ ϕ↔ψ: True if ϕ have the same truth value.

5. **Quantifiers:**

   - **The meaning of a formula depends on the scope of quantifiers:**
   - ❖ **Universal Quantifier (∀):** ∀xϕ(x) is true if ϕ(x) is true for all x in the domain.
   - ❖ Example: ∀x(Human(x)→Mortal(x)): True if every human in the domain is mortal.
   - ❖ **Existential Quantifier (∃):** ∃xϕ(x) is true if ϕ(x) is true for at least one x in the domain.
   - ❖ Example: ∃xLoves(x,Mary): True if at least one individual loves Mary.

Examples of Semantics in FOL

1. **Example 1: Simple Interpretation**

   - Domain: {Suryanaryana, Suryakanthammma, Kameswari
   - **Interpretation:**
   - ❖ Loves(x,y): True if x loves y.
   - ❖ Loves(Suryanarayana, Suryakanthamma) = True

2. **Sentence Evaluation:**

    - **Loves(John,Mary): True (as defined in the interpretation).**
    - **∃xLoves(x,Mary): True (since John loves Mary)**

Example 2: Quantifier Scope

3. **Sentence: ∀x∃yLoves(x,y):**
    - ❖ Meaning: "Everyone loves someone."
    - ❖ Interpretation: True if for every individual x, there exists at least one y such that Loves(x,y) is true.

Importance of Semantics in FOL

1. **Consistency and Truth:**

    - Semantics ensures that sentences are interpreted consistently based on the domain and interpretation.
    - This prevents ambiguities in reasoning.

2. **Knowledge Representation:**

    - FOL semantics allows precise representation of facts, rules, and relationships in AI systems.

3. **Automated:**

    - Semantics underpins logical inference, enabling systems to deduce new facts from existing knowledge.

4. **Problem-Solving in FOL Semantics:**

    - By defining clear semantics, FOL enables AI systems to solve problems involving constraints, relationships, and objectives.

5. **Natural Language Understanding:**

    - Mapping natural language to FOL requires an understanding of semantics to preserve meaning.

Summary: The semantics of First-Order Logic (FOL) form the basis for interpreting and evaluating logical sentences. By defining a domain, assigning meanings to constants, predicates, and functions, and using logical connectives and quantifiers, semantics ensures that FOL representations are meaningful and accurate/correct. This makes FOL an essential tool for reasoning, knowledge representation, and the creation of clever AI systems.

Inference in First Order Logic: Propositional Versus First Order Inference:

Inference in logic involves deriving new conclusions from a set of premises or facts using formal reasoning rules. In **First-Order Logic (FOL)**, inference extends the capabilities of propositional logic by incorporating objects, relationships, and quantifiers, making it more expressive and versatile.

This section explores the differences and capabilities of **propositional inference** versus **first-order inference**.

1. Propositional Inference

Propositional inference operates on statements (propositions) that are either true or false. It is based on the rules of **propositional logic** and does not involve objects, quantifiers, or relationships.

Characteristics:

1. **Fixed Propositions:**

   - Works with atomic propositions like P, Q, R, which represent fixed truths.
   - Example: P: "It is raining.

2. **Inference Rules:**

   - Inference is performed using rules like Modus Ponens, Modus Tollens, and Resolution.
   - **Example (Modus Ponens):**
     ❖ Premise 1: P→QP.

- ❖ Premise 2: P.
- ❖ Conclusion: Q.

3. **No Quantifiers:**

    - Propositional logic cannot express statements involving "for all" (∀) or "there exists" (∃).

4. **Limited Expressiveness:**

    - Propositional inference cannot represent relationships between objects or handle dynamic scenarios effectively.
    - Example: Propositional logic cannot express "All humans are mortal."

5. **First-Order Inference**

First-order inference extends propositional inference by incorporating objects, relationships, and quantifiers, enabling reasoning about structured knowledge.

Characteristics:

1. **Objects and Relationships:**

    - Works with predicates like Human(x) or Loves(x,y), which represent properties or relationships.
    - Example: Mortal(x): "x is mortal."

2. **Quantifiers:**

    - Uses universal quantifiers (∀) and existential quantifiers (∃\\ to express general or specific truths.
    - Example:
    - ❖ ∀x(Human(x)→Mortal(x)) "All humans are mortal."
    - ❖ ∃xLoves(John,x): "John loves someone."

3. **Inference Rules:**

   - Includes specialized inference techniques like unification, substitution, forward chaining, backward chaining, and resolution in the presence of quantifiers.

   - Example (Unification):
     - Loves(John,y) and Loves(John,Mary) Unified by y=Mary.

4. **Higher Expressiveness:**

   - First-order inference allows reasoning about dynamic, structured scenarios involving relationships, constraints, and complex conditions.

Propositional vs. First-Order Inference:
Propositional inference deals with specific cases, while first-order inference generalizes and applies to broader domains. In table 5.2 elaborates the comparison of features between propositional and first-order inference,

Importance of First-Order Inference in AI

1. **Expressiveness:**

   - Allows reasoning about structured knowledge involving objects, relationships, and quantifiers.

Table 5.2 Propositional Inference and First-Order Inference

Feature	Propositional Inference	First-Order Inference
1. Nature and Expressiveness	Simple atomic statements; logical connectives (AND, OR, NOT, IF-THEN)	Predicates, quantifiers, variables, functions, constants; can express relationships and generalizations
2. Expressiveness and Limitations	Limited to specific facts; can't capture internal structure	Complex relationships and general rules; can't quantify over predicates

3. Inference Rules	Modus Ponens, Modus Tollens, Resolution; Truth tables	Includes propositional rules plus Universal/Existential Instantiation and Generalization
4. Computational Complexity	NP-complete (SAT); generally, faster for small/medium problems	Undecidable in general; can be intractable for large domains
5. Decidability	Decidable and complete	Semi-decidable and incomplete (Gödel's theorems)
6. Knowledge Representation	Suitable for simple, specific facts; finite domains	Better for general knowledge, rules, complex relationships; infinite domains
7. Reasoning Capabilities	Limited to logical combinations of known facts	Can reason about classes of objects and general properties
8. Practical Applications	Circuit design, basic expert systems, SAT solvers	NLP, complex knowledge bases, automated theorem proving, planning
9. Learning Curve and Implementation	Easier to understand and implement	More advanced concepts; complex implementation
10. Inference Algorithms	DPLL, CDCL for SAT solving	Resolution with unification, Tableaux methods, Herbrand's theorem
11. Handling of Uncertainty	Can extend with probabilistic models; limited for general statements	Probabilistic first-order logics; better for complex, relational domains
12. Scalability	Good for limited propositions; can become unwieldy for many	Better for general rules; can handle infinite domains but may face computational challenges

Abbreviations:
- **NP-complete SAT**: Non-deterministic Polynomial-time Complete Boolean Satisfiability Problem
- **CDCL**: Conflict-Driven Clause Learning
- **DPLL**: Davis-Putnam-Logemann-Loveland

2. **Scalability:**
   - Facilitates reasoning in complex, dynamic domains such as semantic web, natural language understanding, and knowledge graphs.

3. **Automation:**
   - Supports automated reasoning and knowledge discovery in AI systems.

4. **Generalization:**
   - Enables AI agents to generalize rules and apply them to new instances.

5. **Versatility:**
   - Essential for tasks like planning, theorem proving, and problem-solving in intelligent systems.

Specialized Inference Techniques in First-Order Logic (FOL)

First-order inference encompasses various specialized techniques designed to handle the complexity of reasoning with quantifiers, predicates, and objects. These techniques—such as unification, substitution, forward chaining, backward chaining, and resolution—enable AI systems to effectively derive conclusions from structured knowledge. The following table provides a concise overview of these techniques, including their descriptions and examples, highlighting their relevance in AI agent contexts. In table 5.3 specialise techniques used in FOL is presented.

Table 5.3 Specialised Techniques used in FOL

Technique	Description	Example
Unification	A process of making two logical expressions identical by finding a suitable mapping of variables.	Unifying Loves (John, x) and Loves (John, Mary) results in x=Mary.
Substitution	Replacing variables with constants or other terms in a logical formula based on a unifier.	Substituting x=Mary in Loves(John,x) gives Loves(John,Mary).
Forward Chaining	A data-driven inference method where rules are applied to known facts to derive new facts.	From Human(Socrates) and $\forall x(Human(x) \rightarrow Mortal(x))$, infer Mortal(Socrates).
Substitution	Replacing variables with constants or other terms in a logical formula based on a unifier.	Substituting x=Mary in Loves(John,x) gives Loves(John, Mary).
Forward Chaining	A data-driven inference method where	From Human(Socrates) and $\forall x(Human(x) \rightarrow Mortal(x))$, infer Mortal(Socrates).

	rules are applied to known facts to derive new facts.	
Backward Chaining	A goal-driven inference method that starts with a query and works backward to find supporting facts.	To prove Mortal(Socrates) and ∀x(Human(x)→Mortal(x)).
Resolution	A rule of inference for automated theorem proving, combining clauses to eliminate variables and derive conclusions.	Resolving ¬Human(Socrates)∨Mortal(Socratess) with Human(Socrates) Mortal(Socrates).

Unification, Forward Chaining, Backward Chaining, Resolution.

Unification
Unification in Artificial Intelligence (AI) refers to the process of integrating multiple domains, such as computer vision, natural language processing, and robotics, into a cohesive framework. From a mathematical perspective, unification involves creating systems that generalise across tasks. In logic, unification plays a critical role, especially in first-order logic (FOL), where it is used to match formulas by finding common substitutions.

Unification refers to two interconnected concepts:
1. **Domain Integration**: The process of combining various AI domains—such as computer vision, natural language processing, robotics, and decision-making—into a cohesive framework. This approach aims to create systems capable of handling tasks across multiple cognitive domains, promoting generalization and interoperability.

2. **Logical Unification**: A mathematical process, particularly in **First-Order Logic (FOL)**, where formulas are matched by finding substitutions that make them identical. Logical unification is fundamental to reasoning, automated theorem proving, and rule-based inference systems.

3. Unification is a process of making two different logical atomic expressions identical by finding a substitution. Unification depends on the substitution process.

4. It takes two literals as input and makes them identical using substitution.

5. Let Ψ_1 and Ψ_2 be two atomic sentences and ? be a unifier such that, $\Psi_1? = \Psi_2?$, then it can be expressed as UNIFY(Ψ_1, Ψ_2)

Unification as Domain Integration
The goal of unification in AI is to move beyond specialized systems designed for narrow tasks (e.g., chatbots for conversation or algorithms for image recognition) and develop **general-purpose AI systems**. These systems integrate multiple domains into a unified architecture capable of performing diverse tasks cohesively.

Key Features:

- Multi-Task Learning: A single system trained to perform tasks across domains, such as combining language understanding with visual perception.

- General Intelligence: Emulating human-like capabilities to perceive, reason, and act seamlessly across multiple contexts.

- Interoperability: Facilitating communication and data exchange between different AI systems to enhance overall functionality.

An AI system that can analyze an image, describe its content using natural language, and then decide actions based on the description (e.g., a robot navigating a room while describing obstacles).

Unification in Logical Systems

Logical unification in AI focuses on matching formulas in reasoning systems. It plays a critical role in **First-Order Logic (FOL)**, where the goal is to find substitutions for variables that make logical expressions identical.

Key Features:

- Matching Variables: Ensuring predicates or terms align by substituting variables with constants or other terms.

- Automated Reasoning: Enabling logical inferences, theorem proving, and resolving queries in knowledge-based systems.

Example

- To unify Loves(Susheela) and Loves(Subbaiah), substitute x for Subbaiah and y with Susheela. Loves (Subbaiah and Susheela)

The Vision of Unified AI

Unification in AI reflects the aspiration for **Artificial General Intelligence (AGI)**, where a single system can:

1. **Perceive**: Understand and interpret data from diverse modalities like images, text, and speech.
2. **Reason**: Make logical decisions based on integrated knowledge across domains.
3. **Act**: Execute actions cohesively in real-world environments.

This vision mirrors human intelligence, striving for systems that can generalize across tasks and domains, providing cohesive and adaptive functionality.

Benefits of Unification in AI
1. **Scalability**: Unified systems reduce redundancy by sharing models and resources across domains.
2. **Interdisciplinary Synergy**: Combines strengths of various AI domains to achieve better outcomes (e.g., combining NLP and vision for multi-modal applications).
3. **Path to General Intelligence**: Brings AI closer to human-like intelligence capable of understanding and acting in diverse environments.

Unification in AI represents the convergence of domain integration and logical reasoning, paving the way for systems that are both versatile and powerful.

Applications of Unification in Modern AI
Unification plays a vital role in advancing modern AI across various domains, enabling systems to integrate knowledge, process multi-modal data, transfer learning across tasks, and perform automated reasoning.

1. Knowledge Integration
Unification facilitates the combination of diverse knowledge sources into coherent systems, enhancing reasoning and decision-making capabilities.

- **Combining Multiple Knowledge Bases** :
  - Merges information from different domains or repositories to create unified systems.
  - Example: Integrating medical knowledge from different databases for comprehensive diagnosis systems.

- **Resolving Conflicts Between Ontologies**
  - Identifies and reconciles inconsistencies in terminology and structure across knowledge sources.
  - Example: Aligning terms like "vehicle" and "car" in different datasets for semantic consistency.

- **Creating Coherent Reasoning Systems:**
  - ❖ Develops frameworks that reason across integrated knowledge bases.
  - ❖ Example: AI systems for legal reasoning that unify statutes and case laws.

2. **Multi-Modal Learning**

Unification in multi-modal learning enables systems to process and integrate diverse types of inputs, creating shared representations across modalities.

- **Processing Different Input Types:**
  - ❖ Handles text, images, audio, and other data streams simultaneously.
  - ❖ Example: AI assistants that interpret spoken commands and provide visual responses.

- **Creating Shared Representations:**
  - ❖ Develops unified feature spaces for multi-modal data, enhancing cross-modal understanding.
  - ❖ Example: Mapping images and textual descriptions into a shared vector space.

- **Example:**
  - **CLIP (Contrastive Language-Image Pre-training)**
    - ❖ An AI model that learns joint representations of images and text, enabling tasks like image-caption matching and zero-shot classification.

3. **Transfer Learning**

Unification enables transfer learning by identifying common patterns across domains and tasks, allowing models to apply knowledge from one area to another.

- **Applying Knowledge Across Domains:**
  - ❖ Reduces the need to train models from scratch for every task.
  - ❖ Example: Using a model trained on language data to perform sentiment analysis in a new domain.

- **Identifying Common Patterns:**
  - ❖ Recognizes transferable features that generalize well across tasks.
  - ❖ Example: Features learned from object detection can be applied to activity recognition.

- **Reducing Task-Specific Training:**
  - ❖ Saves computational resources and data by reusing pre-trained models.
  - ❖ Example: BERT (Bidirectional Encoder Representations from Transformers) applied to various NLP tasks with minimal fine-tuning.

4. **Automated Reasoning**

Unification drives logical inference in AI systems, enabling them to solve complex problems using formal reasoning techniques.

- **Theorem Proving**
  - ❖ Uses resolution and logical unification to validate or refute mathematical and logical statements.
  - ❖ Example: Proving mathematical theorems in systems like Coq and Isabelle.

- **Logic Programming:**
  - ❖ Employs unification to resolve queries in rule-based systems like Prolog.
  - ❖ Example: Answering questions based on predefined rules and facts.

- **Constraint Satisfaction :**
  - ❖ Solves problems by finding assignments to variables that satisfy given constraints.
  - ❖ Example: Scheduling tasks or solving Sudoku puzzles.

Examples of Unification in AI

Unification in AI is exemplified by systems that integrate capabilities across multiple domains, enabling cohesive functionality and generalization. Below are notable examples:

1. **OpenAI's GPT-4**

- **Description:**

    OpenAI's GPT-4 embodies unification by integrating diverse capabilities, including text understanding, code generation, and conversational intelligence, into a single model.

- **Significance:**

    GPT-4 demonstrates how a unified AI system can perform a wide range of tasks, from answering questions to generating programming code, while maintaining contextual understanding across applications.

2. **Google DeepMind's Gato**

- **Description:**

    Gato is a general-purpose AI model designed to handle a variety of tasks, such as language translation, robotic control, and image captioning, within a single architecture.

- **Significance:**

    By training on multiple modalities and tasks, Gato showcases how unification can create versatile AI systems capable of functioning seamlessly across diverse domains.

3. Self-Driving Cars

- **Description:**
  Autonomous vehicles exemplify unification by combining computer vision, decision-making algorithms, and sensor fusion to navigate and operate safely in real-world environments.

- **Significance:**
  Self-driving cars integrate data from cameras, LiDAR, GPS, and other sensors into a cohesive system, enabling perception, planning, and execution to work harmoniously for safe and effective autonomous driving.

Conclusion

These examples illustrate the potential of unification in AI to create systems that generalize across domains, providing robust, versatile, and scalable solutions for complex, real-world applications.

Unification is central to modern AI applications, enabling systems to integrate knowledge, learn from multiple modalities, transfer insights across domains, and reason effectively. These capabilities are driving advancements in AI towards more versatile and cohesive systems.

Forward Chaining:

Forward chaining, also known as **forward deduction** or **forward reasoning**, is an inference method used in Artificial Intelligence (AI) to deduce new information from existing facts and rules. It is a **bottom-up approach** that starts with known facts and applies inference rules to derive new conclusions until a specific goal is reached. This method evaluates existing information—facts, derivations, and conditions—stored in the knowledge base and applies logical rules to infer additional facts or reach a decision. Forward chaining is commonly used in **expert systems** and other knowledge-driven AI applications.

How Forward Chaining Works

- **Input: A set of known facts and a knowledge base of inference rules.**
- **Process:**

- ❖ Evaluate facts and identify rules whose premises match these facts.
- ❖ Apply those rules to infer new facts.
- ❖ Repeat the process until no new facts can be deduced or a specific goal is achieved.
- **Output:** A conclusion or decision derived from the chain of logical inferences.

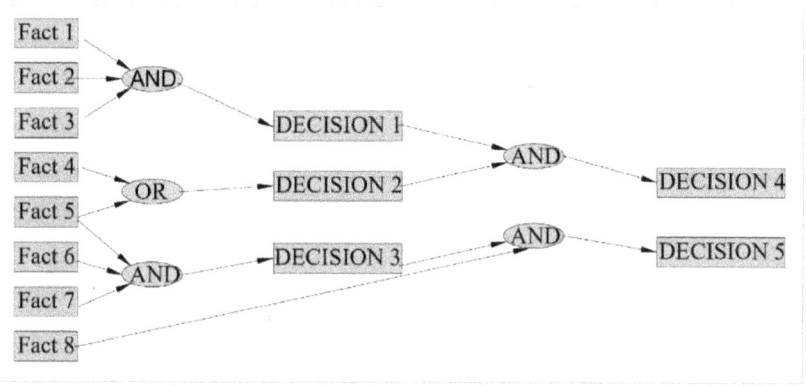

Figure 5.5 Forward Chaining

Example of Forward Chaining

Scenario:

- **Fact 1:** A dog is available for adoption through person A.
- **Fact 2:** Person B is looking to adopt a dog.
- **Inference Rule:**
  - ❖ "If a dog is up for adoption and someone is looking to adopt, that person can adopt the dog."

Process:
1. The system evaluates the known facts:

   - DogAvailable For A dog is available through A.

- LookingToAdopt(B): Person B is looking to adopt.
2. The rule DogAvailableForAdoption(x)∧LookingToAdopt(y)→ CanAdopt(y,x) matches the facts.

- The system applies the rule and infers:

- **CanAdopt(B, A): Person B can adopt the dog from person A.**

Conclusion:

- Person B can adopt the dog from person A This demonstrates how forward chaining deduces new facts and reaches a decision by applying logical rules to known data.

Advantages of Forward Chaining
3. **Goal Independence**: Derives all possible conclusions, making it useful for exploring all consequences of a knowledge base.
4. **Simplicity**: Follows a straightforward, rule-driven approach.
5. **Applicability**: Ideal for systems with a large knowledge base requiring extensive fact exploration, such as medical diagnostics or decision-support systems.

Disadvantages of Forward Chaining
1. **Time-Consuming:**
    - Forward chaining can be computationally expensive because it evaluates all rules repeatedly, even if only a few are relevant. This makes it less efficient for large and complex knowledge bases.

2. **Data Synchronization:**
    - The need to synchronize large volumes of data can slow down the process, particularly when the knowledge base frequently changes or involves distributed systems.

3. **Unclear Fact Explanation:**
    - Forward chaining does not inherently explain *why* a conclusion was reached, as it focuses on generating new facts rather than

providing justifications. This makes it less transparent compared to methods like backward chaining.

4. **Potential for Redundant Inferences:**

    - Forward chaining may repeatedly infer the same facts, wasting computational resources *without contributing new insights.*

5. **Goal Irrelevance**

    - Since forward chaining explores all possible conclusions, it may infer facts that are unrelated to the intended goal, leading to inefficiency.

Addressing Disadvantages
While forward chaining has limitations, these can be mitigated by optimizing rule evaluation, prioritizing relevant facts, and integrating hybrid approaches that combine forward and backward chaining for more targeted reasoning.

Backward Chaining
Backward chaining, backward deduction, or backwards is a reasoning approach that works in the opposite/reverse direction as forward chaining. The approach that is top-down involves drawing judgments or setting objectives to get to the facts. Backward chaining is the process of backtracking usage in diagnostics, debugging, and prescriptions.

- An inference technique that starts with a goal and works backward to see if existing facts and rules can support it. It asks questions based on the goal and searches for premises in rules that match known facts. If matches are found, the corresponding conclusions are added as temporary assumptions, potentially leading to other subgoals.

- **Example:**

  ❖ Goal: "Is the floor wet?"
  ❖ Rule: "The floor will be wet if it's raining and the windows are open."
  ❖ The system asks if it's raining and checks if the windows are open. If both are true, the rule's conclusion ("The floor is wet") becomes a

temporary assumption. Further reasoning might be needed to confirm or refute this assumption based on other rules and facts.

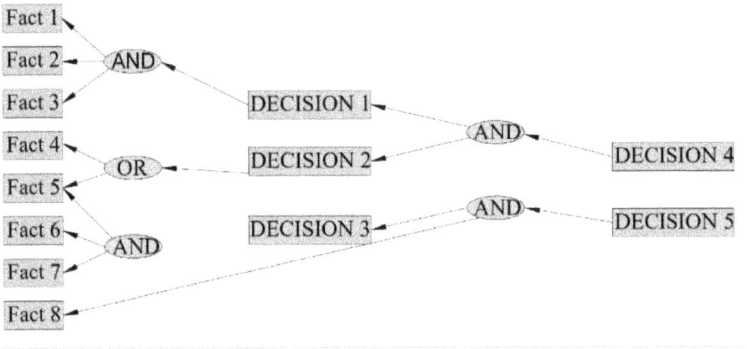

Figure 5.6 Backward Chaining

Advantages and Disadvantages of Backward Chaining

Advantages

1. **Focused Reasoning:**
   - Backward chaining is goal-oriented, allowing the system to focus only on the facts and rules relevant to achieving the specific goal.

2. **Efficiency for Specific Queries Efficiency of Backward Chaining:**
   - It avoids unnecessary exploration of unrelated facts, making it faster for targeted decision-making.

3. **Simpler Process for Known Goals:**
   - The process is straightforward when the endpoint or desired outcome is clearly defined.

4. **Effective Problem Solving:**
   - Backward chaining efficiently drives correct solutions by working systematically from the goal backward through supporting evidence.

Disadvantages:

1. **Single Answer:**
   - Backward chaining typically provides only one solution to the query, even if alternative solutions may exist.

2. **Less Flexibility:**
   - The method is rigidly tied to the defined goal, making it unsuitable for exploring a broad range of possibilities.

3. **Dependence on Known Endpoints Known Endpoints in Backward Chaining:**
   - It works best when the desired endpoint or conclusion is already known, limiting its applicability in open-ended problem-solving.

4. **Complex Execution:**
   - For large and complex knowledge bases, backward chaining can become challenging to execute due to the potential need for deep recursive searches.

Choosing Backward Chaining

Backward chaining is particularly well-suited for **diagnostic systems**, **planning tasks**, and **decision support tools**, where specific outcomes or conclusions are sought. While it is efficient and focused, its limitations make it less applicable to problems requiring exploration of multiple solutions or open-ended reasoning.

Resolution in Artificial Intelligence (AI)

Resolution is a powerful rule of inference used in **logic-based AI systems** to deduce new facts, resolve contradictions, and prove the validity of logical statements. It operates primarily in the context of **First-Order Logic (FOL)** and **Propositional Logic**, playing a central role in **automated theorem proving** and **logical reasoning**. Resolution simplifies complex logical expressions and is integral to the design of SAT solvers and knowledge-based systems.

Key Concepts of Resolution

5. Proof by Contradiction:
Resolution is based on the principle of proof by contradiction. To prove a hypothesis H, assume ¬H derive a contradiction (an empty clause ∅).

6. Clauses and Literals:
- Resolution operates on clauses, which are disjunctions of literals (atomic propositions or their negations).
- Example: P∨¬QP is a clause with literals P and ¬Q.

7. Conjunctive Normal Form (CNF):
- All logical expressions must be converted to CNF, where a formula is expressed as a conjunction of disjunctions.
- Example: (P∨Q)∧(¬Q∨R).

8. Resolution Rule:
- The resolution rule combines two clauses that contain complementary literals to derive a new clause.
- Example: From P∨QP and ¬Q∨R, resolve Q and ¬Q to derive P∨R.

Steps in Resolution

1. Convert to CNF:
- Rewrite the logical formula in Conjunctive Normal Form.

2. Negate the Hypothesis:
- If proving H, assume ¬H and add it to the clauses.

3. Apply the Resolution Rule:
- Iteratively resolve pairs of clauses to derive new clauses.

4. **Check for Contradictions:**

   - If an empty clause ∅ is derived, the hypothesis H is proven true.

Example of Resolution in AI:
Problem:

Prove that Socrates is mortal using the following facts and rules:

1. Human(Jagannadh): "Jagannadh is human."
2. ∀x (Human(x) → Mortal(x)): "All humans are mortal."

Steps:

1. **Convert to CNF:**

   - Human(Jagannadh): Already in CNF.
   - ∀x(Human(x)→Mortal(x: Rewrite as ¬Human(x)∨Mortal(x).

2. **Negate the Hypothesis:**

   - Hypothesis: Mortal(Jagannadh).
   - **Negate it: ¬Mortal(Jagannadh).**

3. **Apply Resolution:**
   - Clause 1: Human(Jagannadh).
   - Clause 2: ¬Human(x)∨Mortal(x) Mortal(x) (instantiate x=Jagannadh to get ¬Human(Jagannadh)∨Mortal(Jagannadh).
   - Clause 3: ¬Mortal(Jagannadh).
   - Resolve Human(Jagannadh) and ¬Human(Jagannadh)∨Mortal(Socrates: Mortal(Socrates).
   - Resolve Mortal(Socrates) and ¬Mortal(Socrates: ∅.

Conclusion:
The empty clause ∅ indicates a contradiction, proving that Socrates is mortal.

Applications of Resolution in AI

1. **Automated Theorem Proving Theorem Proving in AI:**
   - Used to verify logical statements and prove mathematical theorems in systems like Coq, Prover9, and Isabelle.

2. **SAT Solvers:**
   - Integral to solving the Boolean Satisfiability Problem (SAT) in systems like DPLL and CDCL.

3. **Knowledge-Based Systems:**
   - Enables reasoning in expert systems by deriving new facts from existing knowledge bases.

4. **Logic Programming:**
   - Powers rule-based languages like Prolog to resolve queries using predefined rules and facts.

5. **Natural Language Processing (NLP) Resolution in NLP:**
   - Facilitates reasoning about textual information by converting natural language statements into logical expressions.

6. **Constraint Satisfaction:**
   - Solves problems like scheduling and resource allocation by resolving constraints iteratively.

Advantages of Resolution:

1. **Systematic and Complete:**
   - Guarantees a solution if one exists, making it reliable for refutation-based proofs.

2. **Uniform Representation:**
   - Operates on a standardized format (CNF), simplifying the inference process.

3. **Wide Applicability:**
   - Effective for both propositional and first-order logic, enabling its use across diverse AI applications.

Limitations of Resolution

1. **Computational Complexity:**
   - Can be computationally expensive for large and complex problems due to clause explosion.

2. **Dependence on CNF:**

Converting logical formulas to CNF can increase the problem's size, complicating the reasoning process.

3. **Focus on Refutation:**
   - Works best for proving contradictions but does not inherently support constructive proofs or explanations.

Resolution is a cornerstone of reasoning in AI, enabling systems to infer, validate, and deduce new knowledge systematically. Despite its computational challenges, its robustness and versatility make it indispensable for applications in theorem proving, SAT solving, knowledge-based systems, and beyond.

Chapter Summary and Concluding Thoughts

In this chapter, we delved upon the fundamental ideas of knowledge-based agents and how they might use stored knowledge to arrive at judgments in dynamic environments. By examining the **Wumpus World**, we illustrated how agents reason under uncertainty, employing logical principles to a navigate and to avoid hazards and achieve/arrive at desired goals.

We covered the basic principles of **logic and propositional logic**, including how logical systems and reasoning patterns serve as the foundation for structured problem solving. This naturally led to a comprehensive discussion on **First-Order Logic (FOL),** where we explored its syntax, semantics, and AI applications for describing complicated relationships and reasoning about objects in a domain.

The chapter concluded with an examination of **inference techniques** such as **unification, forward chaining, backward chaining, and resolution**, highlighting their applications in propositional and first-order instances. These strategies enable AI agents to acquire new knowledge, validate hypotheses, and make intelligent decisions.

Together, these topics provide an in-depth/comprehensive understanding of how knowledge representation, logical reasoning, and inference methods support intelligent systems, laying the foundation for advanced AI applications.

Chapter Wise Questions

Chapter 1: Artificial Intelligence (AI): Foundations and History

Questions for Review:
1. Define Artificial Intelligence (AI). How does it aim to mimic human thinking and behaviour?
2. What are the foundational disciplines that contribute to the development of AI, and how does each play a role?
3. Explain the significance of natural language processing (NLP) in the evolution of AI. Provide examples of its application in daily life.
4. Discuss the importance of machine learning in the growth of AI. How does it differ from traditional programming?
5. What role does computer vision play in AI, and what are some examples of its impact on industries?
6. How has AI evolved from its early fundamental principles to its present-day applications by 2024?
7. Describe the role of robotics in AI. How does it integrate with other fields like computer science and engineering?
8. Explain how AI is transforming industries and influencing everyday life. Provide at least two examples.
9. What are the historical milestones in the development of AI, and how have they shaped its current state?
10. In your own words, summarize the interdisciplinary nature of AI and its potential to drive future innovations.

Chapter 2: Agents and Environments

Questions for Review:

1. Define an intelligent agent and describe the relationship between an agent and its environment. How do they interact?

2. What is the concept of rationality in the context of intelligent agents? How is it used to evaluate an agent's performance?

3. Explain the different types of environments in which intelligent agents operate. How do properties like observability, determinism, and continuity influence the design of agents?

4. Discuss the structure of agents. What are the key components that make up an intelligent agent?

5. How do simple reflex agents differ from model-based agents? Provide examples to illustrate the differences.

6. What are chatbots, and how do they function as intelligent agents? Give examples of their practical applications.

7. Describe expert systems (ES). What are their main components, and how do they assist in decision-making?

8. What is the role of domain knowledge in expert systems? How is it represented and used effectively?

9. Explain the concept of expert system shells. How do they simplify the development of expert systems?

10. Discuss the process of knowledge acquisition in expert systems. Why is it considered a critical challenge in developing ES?

Chapter 3: Uncertain Knowledge and Reasoning

Questions for Review:
1. Why is quantifying uncertainty important in AI, and how does it enable agents to reason and act effectively in uncertain environments?
2. Define the term "uncertainty" in the context of AI. Provide examples of situations where uncertainty plays a key role.
3. Explain the concept of acting under uncertainty. What challenges do AI agents face in such scenarios?
4. What is basic probability notation, and how is it used to represent uncertain events in AI systems?
5. Discuss the importance of inference using full joint distributions. How do they help in reasoning about multiple variables in uncertain systems?
6. What is the principle of independence in probability theory? How does it simplify the representation and computation of probabilities?
7. State Bayes' Rule. How does it help in updating beliefs based on new evidence?
8. Provide an example of how Bayes' Rule is applied in real-world AI applications, such as spam filtering or medical diagnosis.
9. What are the differences between probability theory and decision theory? How are they integrated in AI for decision-making under uncertainty?
10. Describe how independence assumptions are leveraged by AI developers to simplify the design of systems that handle uncertainty. Why are these assumptions critical for scalability?

Chapter 4: Search Strategies and Logical Agents

Questions for Review:
1. What is the role of search strategies in problem-solving agents, and why are they essential for navigating problem spaces?
2. Differentiate between uninformed and informed search strategies. Provide examples of each type and discuss their applications.
3. Explain the concept of a problem-solving agent. How does it approach finding solutions in a given problem space?
4. What are the key differences between Breadth-First Search (BFS) and Depth-First Search (DFS)? Discuss their advantages and limitations.
5. Describe the Iterative Deepening Depth-First Search (IDDFS) strategy. Why is it considered a hybrid approach, and what are its advantages?
6. What is a heuristic function in the context of informed search strategies? How does it guide the search process?
7. Explain the Greedy Best-First Search strategy. What are its strengths and weaknesses, and how does it rely on heuristics?
8. Discuss the A Search algorithm. How does it combine the concepts of cost and heuristics to find optimal solutions? *
9. Provide examples of real-world problems that can be solved using search strategies. How do these strategies contribute to finding efficient solutions?
10. What are logical agents, and how do they differ from problem-solving agents in their approach to decision-making and reasoning?

Chapter 5: Knowledge-Based Agents and Logical Reasoning

Questions for Review:
1. What is a knowledge-based agent, and how does it use stored knowledge to make decisions and solve problems?

2. Describe the Wumpus World environment. How does it serve as a classic example for reasoning under uncertainty?

3. What are the key differences between propositional logic and first-order logic (FOL)? Provide examples of each.

4. Explain the syntax and semantics of first-order logic (FOL). How do they contribute to the expressive power of FOL compared to propositional logic?

5. What are reasoning patterns in propositional logic? Discuss their significance in AI problem-solving.

6. Define unification in the context of first-order logic. Why is it critical for logical inference?

7. What is forward chaining, and how does it work in first-order logic? Provide an example of its application.

8. Explain backward chaining as a reasoning technique. How does it differ from forward chaining in its approach?

9. Discuss the resolution method in first-order logic. How does it enable inference, and why is it important in AI systems?

10. Compare and contrast propositional inference and first-order inference. What are the strengths and limitations of each?

Index

A

A* Search Algorithm 102, 122, 130
Abductive Reasoning 146
Acting Humanly 7, 8
Acting Rationally 7, 8
Adaptive Intelligence 5
Agent ... x, 1, 19, 21, 22, 30, 32, 33, 34, 35, 37, 41, 44, 50, 51, 54, 57, 62, 63, 93, 94, 95, 100, 134, 136, 141, 193, 194, 195
AlphaGo 15
Artificial Intelligence (AI) . 1, 86, 98, 114, 122, 167, 174, 179, 185, 193
Autonomous systems 50

B

Backward Chaining ...... x, 133, 137, 143, 167, 177, 178, 179
Bayesian Inference..................... 83
Breadth-First Search (BFS) 102, 104, 107, 111, 120, 122, 129, 132, 188

C

Chatbot .... x, 65, 193, 194
Cognitive Science 30, 193
computer vision 167, 168, 174, 185
Conditional probability 83
Conjunctive Normal Form (CNF) 180
Constants 151, 155, 158

Control Theory 30
Convolutional Neural Networks. 16

D

decision theory . 30, 77, 86, 97, 187
Deep Learning ... 9, 11, 16, 193, 194
Depth-First Search (DFS). 102, 105, 109, 111, 115, 122, 129, 132, 188
Depth-Limited Search (DLS) 109, 111
Dialogue Management 66
Domain of Discourse................ 158
Dynamic Environments 78

E

Episodic...................................... 59
expert system 67, 68, 186

F

First-Order Logic (FOL).... 144, 150, 155, 157, 161, 165, 168, 169, 179, 184
Forward Chaining. x, 133, 137, 143, 166, 167, 174, 175, 176
Fully Observable Environment. 194

G

General AI (AGI) 10
Generative AI 15
Goal-Based Agent 195

Greedy Best-First Search (GBFS)
............................102, 119, 132

H

heuristic function.....119, 120, 121, 125, 130, 188
Human-AI Collaboration 27

I

independence 76, 86, 92, 94, 97, 187
Inductive Reasoning................. 145
Inference...... xi, 70, 74, 76, 90, 133, 134, 137, 138, 139, 149, 161, 162, 163, 164, 165, 175
Informed Search 98, 99, 102
intelligent agent....57, 78, 134, 186
Iterative Deepening Depth-First Search (IDDFS). x, 102, 104, 109, 111, 112, 132, 188

J

joint probability ..76, 90, 91, 92, 93

K

Knowledge Engineer 68
Knowledge-Based Agents 134, 138, 189

L

Large Language Models (LLMs..... 9
Learning Agents 43
Limited Memory 10
Logical connectives 149, 155
Logical Connectives ..... x, 146, 152, 155, 159

M

Machine learning 195
Model-Based Agent 195
Multi-agent systems 51
Multidisciplinary Approach.......... 4

N

Natural Language Processing 9, 46, 66, 85, 96, 182, 194
Neural network.............4, 9, 11, 15

P

Partially Observable Environment
.... 194
PEAS framework...................... 142
Perception 5, 6, 26, 32, 35, 41
predicates 153, 154, 155, 161, 162, 163, 165, 169
Problem-solving agents 99, 126
Propositional Logic........x, 133, 144, 146, 148, 179

Q

Quantifiers........152, 155, 159, 162

R

Rationality 27
Reactive Machines..................... 10
reflex agents 31, 33, 34, 64, 186
Reinforcement Learning 13, 45, 80, 195
Resolution..53, 133, 161, 164, 167, 179, 180, 181, 182, 183
Robotics ..4, 5, 37, 46, 96, 114, 122

S

search strategies ..98, 99, 104, 126, 132, 188
Self-Aware 11
Semantics ..133, 157, 158, 159, 160
sensors ... 26, 35, 40, 61, 62, 63, 75, 78, 174
Sequential 60
Simple Reflex Agents 31
State Space Representation 99, 100
Stochastic Environment 195
Super AI (ASI) 10
Supervised 11, 12, 45, 195
Supervised Learning 12, 45, 195
Swarm intelligence 56
Syntax 133, 154, 155

T

training data 67
Training Data 67
Transformer architecture 16

U

uncertainty ... 30, 35, 38, 39, 59, 74, 75, 76, 77, 78, 79, 80, 81, 82, 84, 85, 86, 90, 92, 94, 95, 97, 139, 140, 145, 184, 187, 189, 195
Uninformed Search 98, 99, 101
Unsupervised Learning .13, 46, 195
Utility Function 40, 43
utility-based agents 40

V

variables.. xi, 57, 75, 82, 83, 90, 91, 92, 94, 96, 147, 154, 155, 156, 163, 166, 167, 169, 173, 187

W

Well-Formed Formulas 155, 156
Wumpus world 133

Glossary

A

- Agent: An autonomous entity in AI capable of perceiving its environment, reasoning, learning, and acting. See also: Multi-Agent System.

- Artificial Intelligence (AI): Simulation of human intelligence in machines programmed to think, learn, and adapt. See also: Deep Learning, NLP.

C

- Chatbot: AI-powered software designed to simulate conversations with human users via text or voice. See also: NLP.

- Cognitive Science: The interdisciplinary study of mind and intelligence, including psychology, neuroscience, and AI.

D

- Deep Learning: A subset of machine learning using neural networks for complex pattern recognition. See also: Neural Network.

- Decision Theory: A framework for rational decision-making in uncertain environments.

E

- Expert System: AI programs that emulate human expertise for decision-making and problem-solving. See also: Utility-Based Agent.

F

- Fully Observable Environment: An environment where an agent has complete access to all relevant information at any given time. See also: Partially Observable Environment.

G

- Goal-Based Agent: An agent that evaluates actions based on their ability to achieve specific objectives. See also: Utility-Based Agent.

L

- Learning Agent: An AI system that improves performance over time by learning from past experiences.

M

- Model-Based Agent: An AI agent that uses an internal model to handle partially observable environments. See also: Reflex Agent.
- Multi-Agent System: A collection of autonomous agents interacting to achieve individual or collective goals. See also: Agent.

N

- Natural Language Processing (NLP): The branch of AI focused on interaction between computers and human language. See also: Chatbot.
- Neural Network: A computational model inspired by the human brain, used extensively in deep learning. See also: Deep Learning.

P

- Partially Observable Environment: An environment where an agent has limited information about the current state. See also: Fully Observable Environment.

R

- Reinforcement Learning: Machine learning where agents learn optimal behavior through rewards and penalties. See also: Supervised Learning, Unsupervised Learning.

- Reflex Agent: An agent that selects actions based on predefined rules, without memory or learning. See also: Model-Based Agent.

S

- Stochastic Environment: An environment that involves randomness and uncertainty in state transitions.

- Supervised Learning: A machine learning approach using labeled data to train models for specific tasks. See also: Unsupervised Learning, Reinforcement Learning.

U

- Unsupervised Learning: A machine learning technique for discovering patterns in data without labeled outputs. See also: Supervised Learning, Reinforcement Learning.

- Utility-Based Agent: An agent that evaluates outcomes using a utility function to select actions maximizing utility. See also: Expert System, Goal-Based Agent.

www.ingramcontent.com/pod-product-compliance
Lightning Source LLC
LaVergne TN
LVHW061545070526
838199LV00077B/6901